Sunset
Dolls
& Soft Toys

By the Editors of Sunset Books
and Sunset Magazine

Lane Publishing Co. • Menlo Park, California

Come play with us...

Come have fun. Meet our carnival of cuddly characters—
Louis Looselimbs, the madcap dancing doll on page 24, for instance, or
our Very Scary Dragon of strokable green fur on page 64. Or maybe the
toy for you is the shocking pink, squishy car on page 72.

This color-filled book will delight you — whether you are making
a toy to enjoy yourself or to give away. You'll find a wide range of huggable
playthings for the young-in-spirit of any age. Sophisticates will enjoy the
life-size Pillow Portraits on page 30. Children will fall in love with just
about everything here. (We know, because we've tried out all our toys
with children.)

For her advice and encouragement in the preparation of this book, we
wish especially to thank Barbara J. Braasch. We also received invaluable
assistance from Althea Bieler, Cranberry Scoop Antiques (Los Altos,
California), Jean Ferris, Charlene Kastigar, Erika Kirtland, Whitney Lane,
Mark Law, Leslie Lievore, Mudpie in the Jester's Eye (Los Altos, California),
Dorcus Ruppert, Joan Schulze, Edena Sheldon, and Marilyn Winslow.

Edited by Susan Warton

Photography: Darrow M. Watt

Design: JoAnn Masaoka

Artwork: Edith Allgood

Cover: Goldibraids (page 26) and our Classic Teddy Bear
(page 62) share the comfortable lap of Ma Pillow, a lifesize
portrait doll (page 31). Photographed by Darrow M. Watt.

Editor, Sunset Books: David E. Clark

Fourth printing August 1985

Beverly Ann Markham
1211 Lenore St.
Johnstown, Pa. 15904

Contents

Getting started

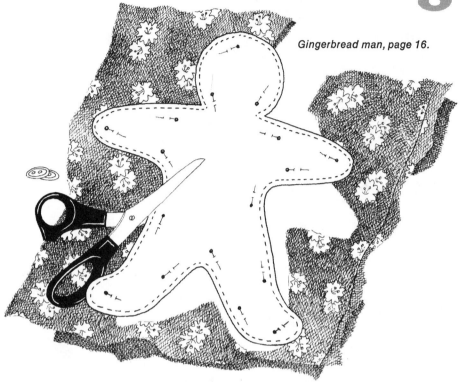

Gingerbread man, page 16.

A comfortable, cuddly toy is often a child's dearest possession. A favorite doll or animal gets hugged, slept on, dragged, and squeezed through the years, long after other toys have been cast aside. Many people save these early friends even into adulthood. Whether passed on to children or tucked away in a cupboard, soft toys seem only to increase in sentimental value—especially if they were lovingly made by hand.

A growing number of people are rediscovering the pleasures of childhood by making soft toys for their children, their grandchildren, their friends' children — or even for themselves. It is fun to create a soft character from fabric, fluff, and trimmings. Soft toy making opens up a wide arena for self-expression. Needlework techniques from patchwork to tatting can be brought into play. Soft toys can be painted, batiked, beaded, or tie-dyed. And here is a chance to indulge in play-acting, portraiture, or parody; to vent a few feelings and fantasies about human nature.

All this takes very little time and money, compared to many crafts. In a few hours or, at most, a few days, you can produce a toy to treasure for years.

Useful tools & supplies

If you have a sewing machine and basic sewing supplies, you're well equipped for making soft toys. When you get right down to it, all you really need are needles, thread, and scissors — toys have been stitched by hand for centuries. But if a machine is available, you'll be grateful for the speed it gives and the sturdy seams it produces.

Listed below are some ingredients of a well-stocked sewing basket. They're not all absolutely essential (some people, for instance, need thimbles; others prefer bare fingers). But you'll find most of these items especially helpful in making soft toys.
- Good sewing shears.
- Embroidery scissors for cutting small pieces.
- Packet of assorted sewing needles.
- Packet of embroidery needles for decorative stitching.
- Packet of assorted large repair needles (including a curved upholstery needle) for hand-stitching with yarn or heavy-duty thread.
- Straight 8-inch needle from an upholstery shop for anchoring button eyes.

- Dental floss, button thread, or quilting thread for handsewing (all three are strong and slick enough to glide through heavy fabric).
- Crochet thread for handsewing (available in many colors at needlework shops).
- Tailor's chalk, dressmaker's carbon paper, and a tracing wheel for transferring patterns.
- Tweezers to help turn small pieces right side out.
- Wooden chopstick or dowel to do the same job, as well as to aid in stuffing.
- Yardstick.
- Tape measure.
- Packet of straight pins.
- Rubber balloon to grip a stubborn needle and pull it through thick fabric.
- Masking tape to bind raw edges of fabric during stuffing.
- White glue or fabric glue for attaching felt features.
- Plastic bags to organize and store scraps and trimmings.

Immensely helpful, too, if you can manage it, is a quiet work space set aside for sewing. Sewing creates a lot of clutter, and it is frustrating to have to clear everything away before you're finished with a project.

If possible, provide yourself with storage space, because as you get deep into toy making you're likely to become a pack rat for fabric, yarn, and trimmings.

Choosing materials

Selecting materials for your toy can be a kind of treasure hunt. Take time to browse, muse, and enjoy it.

Think about the character of your toy and how to convey it with fabric and trim. Elegant tweed gives even a lowly field mouse an air of sophistication. The same mouse in felt or gingham would have an entirely different personality.

Consider what destiny is in store for your toy. For example, if you're making it for a toddler, you should expect it to be given fairly rough treatment. You'll probably want it to be not only cuddly, but also sturdy and washable. And because toddlers taste everything, you may decide to avoid buttons or other small trimmings that might come loose.

Fabrics

Whether you're searching for something specific (like fluffy green fur for a luxurious dragon) or simply collecting ideas for future projects, there are many places to look for fabric. Check the remnant counters of yardage shops; sometimes you can find just the right piece at a reduced price. Many dime stores also stock fabric at moderate prices.

Keep your eyes open at garage sales, thrift shops, flea markets — you may discover what you need in a necktie, kimono, or lace tablecloth. Used winter coats can be revitalized in the form of a cuddly toy. Look through good-but-discarded clothing at home, too. If you save bags of fabric scraps, sort through them for possible trimmings and other materials for doll clothes.

Felt is one of the basic fabrics for toy making. Colorful and nonraveling, it is an excellent choice for appliquéd features and tiny clothing. You can collect an assortment of felt squares or, for large projects, buy felt by the yard in various weights. Though felt won't hold up through repeated washings, a few turns in the machine won't hurt small appliquéd pieces.

Napped fabrics — such as corduroy, velour, and fake fur — lend a luxury of texture (and, of course, a touch of realism if the toy is an animal). Many fluffy fabrics are washable; check the bolt to be sure. Buy enough napped fabrics to allow for laying all the pattern pieces in the same direction; otherwise, your toy will look oddly tousled, and seams will be obvious.

(Continued on next page)

Heavier fabrics are often in short supply during the summer. The best selection of fake fur is usually available in late August or early September.

Stretchy fabrics—knits, stretch terry cloth, scraps from T-shirts, socks, pantyhose, and tights — become incredibly lifelike when sculpted with a few stitches (see page 44). You can't stuff them as firmly as other fabrics, though, so you must expect a rather floppy result.

Closely woven cottons and blends are reliable choices for children's toys and doll clothing. For bodies, use sturdy fabrics that hold their shape (sailcloth, duck, denim, muslin). Crisp, lightweight fabrics are better suited to clothing (remember that prints will look much bigger on the toy than on the bolt). Because seam allowances in toys are usually narrow—¼ to ½ inch—fabrics that fray easily, like cotton flannel or voile, can cause problems.

Be sure to preshrink all washable fabrics before cutting out your toy. Washing will also remove any surface finish (called sizing) from the fabric, making it easier to sew.

Stuffings and fillings

In the past, toys were filled with anything soft that could be found — from rags to cornhusks. Some people still recycle cut-up pantyhose (time-consuming, maybe, but it makes a perfectly good stuffing). By far the most popular material today is polyester fiber. Unlike kapok, commonly used a few years ago, polyester fiber is tidy to work with and machine washable. It is sold in 1-pound bags at fabric and variety stores. For a firmly packed doll about 16 inches high, you would need most of one bag. Polyester fiber also comes in the form of a rolled sheet called batting, commonly used to fill quilts. Batting is sold either by the yard or in 1-pound bags.

Shredded foam (also available at fabric and variety stores) is more economical and might be preferable for a giant-size toy. A foam-filled toy is squeezable and bouncy, but one drawback is that the shreds are fantastically messy. Jumpy with static electricity, they stick to everything. One doll maker's ingenious solution is to strip the bathroom and herself, close the door, and work with the foam in the tub — its drain sealed with masking tape. Afterwards, a quick vacuuming picks up any wayward shreds.

You could also try one of the laundry products that subdue static electricity in machine-dried clothing. Generously spray the inside of a giant plastic bag. Put the unopened package of foam inside, empty the foam, seal the giant bag, and shake well. This should make the shreds more manageable.

Solid blocks of foam are also available (check the Yellow Pages under Rubber — Foam and Sponge). The supplier will usually cut the blocks roughly to size. You can shape them to suit your toy with an electric carving knife, bread knife, or band saw. Use scissors for carving details. See pages 58, 66, and 72 for projects using foam blocks.

Other fillings to consider include cotton wool (compressible, but lumpy after washing), sawdust (light and inexpensive), and sand (useful to steady the base of a toy). Birdseed is an inexpensive bean bag filler. No matter which you choose, a bag of polyester fiber will come in handy as a supplement for smoothly modeled results.

A few basics of toy design

Once you have in mind a picture of your future toy — and have ready at hand all the ingredients — you'll probably itch to start your project. Before you actually cut the cloth, though, consider these guidelines for using the patterns presented here as well as for working out designs of your own.

Pattern transfer

To use the patterns in this book you'll need to enlarge and transfer them to graph paper. First, make a grid of squares by ruling horizontal and vertical lines between the dots that border our patterns. To enlarge a pattern, copy our outline on a larger grid of squares.

At the beginning of each project you'll find the size of the finished toy. A corresponding grid size is indicated on the pattern. In nearly every case, these sizes are arbitrary. You may want a much bigger toy — or a miniature version. If so, just transfer our pattern to a grid with squares that are either larger or smaller than the size we've given. Be careful, though — you need to change the grid only slightly to achieve dramatic differences in size. If you enlarge a pattern from a 1-inch to a 2-inch grid, for example, you'll *quadruple* the size. Any toy you enlarge, of course, will require greater quantities of materials.

You can rule your own grid on wrapping paper or buy graph tracing paper at a stationery or art supply store (the largest printed grid generally available has four squares to the inch). Some fabric shops carry less expensive pattern tissue paper with marks spaced an inch apart. By inter-

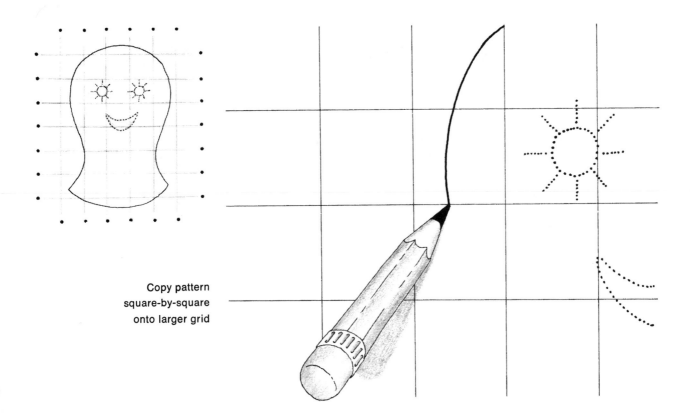

Copy pattern
square-by-square
onto larger grid

secting some or all of them, you can create a 1-inch—or larger—grid.

Copy the pattern carefully, one square at a time (see sketch above). When you finish, you'll have an actual-size pattern ready to cut out. It might be wise, though, to trace the graph paper pattern and use the tracing as a working pattern. This way, you can make the same toy several times or alter it without losing your basic design.

Designing your own

Toy making, like other crafts, opens the door to a world of imaginative adventure. Our projects are meant to inspire you rather than to direct you down a narrow path. As soon as you get your feet wet—or your needle threaded—you'll probably want to create your own designs.

One approach is to think of the doll, animal, or other toy as a pillow—just a front and a back cut from one pattern. Arms and legs can be outlined on the pattern or indicated later with paints, appliqué, or stitchery.

If you want to make a more complicated toy or to alter one of ours, here are some points to consider:

Heads, especially on narrow necks, tend to become wobbly in time as their stuffing settles. One solution is to make a separate head with a good, strong neck. Handstitch it to the finished body

after packing it firmly, adding bits of stuffing right up to the last minute.

Movable arms and legs delight children. Here are three special arm and leg joints you can make to add agility to your toy:

• Sandwich a flat button between the finished body and limb as shown below. If you like, you can slip your needle through a bead on the outside of the arm or leg to hide the stitching. On small toys, a set of snaps creates the same swivel effect.

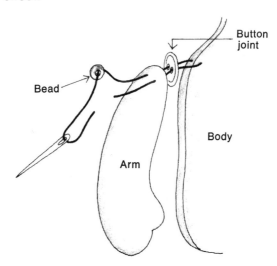

Bead

Button joint

Body

Arm

• Stitch "hinges" across limbs at elbows and knees, and again where the limbs join the body (see Goldibraids, page 26). Stuff the lower portion first; then, using a zipper foot, machine stitch across the limb to hold the stuffing in place. Next, *loosely* stuff the upper portion, leaving an inch or two empty at the top. Stitch body seams, leaving openings for limbs and stuffing. Insert open ends of limbs into unstuffed body and machine stitch to attach them.

• With pairs of jar lids (baby food lids are perfect) you can bolt together swivel joints at hips, upper torso, even the neck (see Teddy Bear on page 62). In the center of each lid, drill or hammer a hole large enough to accommodate matching bolts. Leave an opening in the top of each stuffed arm or leg, as shown in sketch 1 below. Fit one lid inside the limb, the other inside the unstuffed body. Join the two with nuts, washers, and bolts in the order shown in sketch 2. To make a neck joint, stuff the head (which has one seam open 5 inches from the neck). Insert the upper jar lid with bolt and washer, and gather the edge of the neck opening. Pull the gathers tight so that only the end of the bolt shows. Finish by putting the bolt through the body fabric at the neck, the lower lid, and the nut (see sketch 3). Slip your hand through the head opening to hold the bolt as you tighten the joint. Blindstitch the opening closed.

Swivel joints

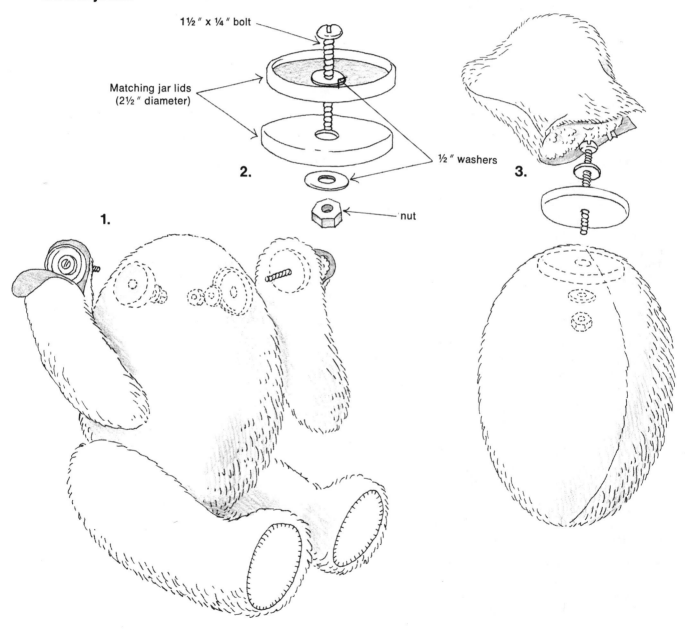

1½ " x ¼ " bolt

Matching jar lids (2½ " diameter)

2.

½ " washers

nut

3.

1.

Doll clothing

Whether you envision a glorious fairy tale gown or just a simple get-up of fabric scraps, you'll find that clothing is fun to design. And it needn't be complicated.

Felt is an easy-to-sew material perfect for heavy doll clothing and shoes. A collection of short lengths of eyelet, wide ruffles, lace, and embroidered ribbon will also come in handy. Old socks and knitted gloves can be cut into tubes and transformed into miniature caps and sweaters—the ribbing provides a nearly ready-made hat brim or turtleneck (see Rabbit, page 49).

Simplest to dress are dolls that never disrobe. You can invent most of their clothing right on their backs, using circles and squares of fabric. For example, you might start with a generous circle: Cut a small hole in the center and a slit in one side of the center hole, making an opening for the doll's head (or cut a large opening which you can later gather tight for a smocked effect). With this poncho-style circle on the doll, carefully snip under the arms and, in flared lines, at the sides. Stitched up, trimmed, and belted (or not), the circle becomes a dress or a tunic (see Ballet Dancers, page 32).

Because armholes on doll clothing are usually too tiny to manage on a sewing machine, you'll need to stitch sleeves to bodice or shirt before sewing sleeve or side seams.

Make full skirts and capes from rectangles of cloth gathered up one long edge.

Narrow, double-fold bias tape finishes raw edges neatly. Use tiny snaps or self-gripping tape for fastenings—unless you want to feature such fascinating gadgets for a young child as zippers, buckles, buttons, and laces (use big ones).

Decorative techniques

Any decorative technique that applies to fabric automatically applies to soft toys, too. A toy can be a kind of sampler, giving you a chance to experiment on a small scale. Often a special decorative approach enhances its charm. Here are just a few possibilities you might like to try:

Paints, pens, and crayons. Large art supply stores carry a variety of pigments designed especially for cloth. You can buy water-base fabric paint in clear, brilliant colors. Use it just like poster paint on prewashed cottons and cotton blends. When the paint dries, set the colors in a hot drier; after that, the fabric can be laundered normally.

You can also buy crayons that "dye" fabric. First draw with them on paper; then lay the draw-

ing face down on the fabric and transfer it by pressing with a warm iron.

Permanent markers and liquid embroidery (pigment in a tube that works like a pen) come in a rainbow of rich colors. Both can produce instant faces, tiger stripes, feathers, whiskers—or any other line drawing that will enliven a toy.

Embroidery. Stitches made of embroidery floss or fine yarn add luster and texture to toys. Needlework shops and some large fabric stores carry a splendid array of colors to choose from. Both yarn and floss come in strands that you can separate for stitches of varying thickness. Take into consideration whether or not your toy needs to be washable: some yarns are not.

For several reasons, stitchery on toys is usually added after sewing and stuffing. The underside of a stitch is less likely to show through the fabric if it is masked by a bit of stuffing. Also, if you embroider before sewing seams—and your seams are slightly inaccurate—the embroidery will no longer be centered.

An embroidered face can look both elegant and cheerful. But don't stop with the face. Experiment with stitches as you design other features—the mane of a lion, the scales of a dragon, or the borders of appliquéd building blocks. Some useful stitches are shown on the next page.

Machine embroidery. With a little experimentation, you can quickly produce exciting embroidery using your sewing machine (see the dolls on page 30 and the mobile on page 75 for examples of this technique). Many machines produce a variety of zigzag stitches; some even do programmed embroidery. But even if your machine

Embroidery Stitches

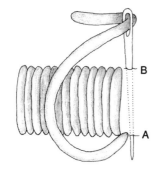

1. Satin stitch

Come up at A; go in at B.
Come up again very close to A
and go in close to B, keeping
stitches even and smooth.

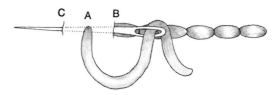

2. Outline stitch

Come up at A; go in at B; come up again at C. Repeat,
going back into same hole at A as the last stitch. Keep
stitches uniform in size.

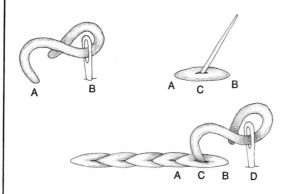

4. Split stitch

Come up at A; go in at B; come up at C, piercing
center of stitch, splitting it in middle.
Go in at D, a little ahead of B.

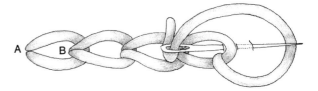

5. Chain stitch

Bring needle up at A. Form a loop and hold thread down with
thumb. Go in again next to A; come up at B. Draw needle over
loop. Do not pull thread tight.

does only straight stitching, take time to play with its embroidery potential. In Mexico, dresses, shirts, and blouses are beautifully decorated on straight-stitch treadle machines.

To find out what your machine can do, review the manual that came with it. Adjust the thread tension and stitch size, and experiment on fabric scraps until you arrive at an effect that pleases you. You might also like to try novelty threads—wind the bobbin by hand and stitch with the fabric face down so that the bobbin thread shows on the right side.

For free motion embroidery and "satin stitch" filling, remove the presser foot (but lower its lever anyway) and lower the feed dog or cover it with a darning plate. To create line drawing, set stitch length and width at zero and keep the fabric as taut as possible as you stitch; a machine

embroidery hoop is helpful here, but it may be hard to find. Move the fabric back and forth under the needle. With a little practice, you'll be delighted at how easily and effectively you can embroider by machine.

Appliqué. Borrowed from the French word for "applied," appliqué is the technique of sewing a piece of fabric to a contrasting background. You can create various effects by using a simple running stitch, embroidery, or decorative machine stitching to attach the design. You can also simply glue down an appliqué (use white glue or one of the fabric glues available at yardage shops). With the exception of those made of felt, most appliqués must be hemmed. Staystitch ⅛ to ¼ inch (depending on the size of the piece) from the edge. Clip curves as needed and press

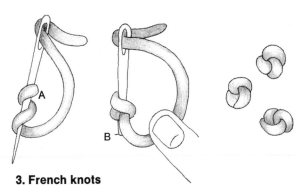

3. French knots

Come up at A. Hold needle close to fabric and coil thread tightly around needle two or three times. Insert needle at B, close to A, keeping thread taut with fingers of free hand.

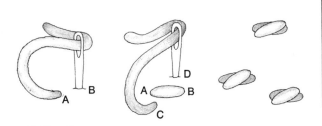

6. Seeding

Come up at A; go in at B a short distance away; pull through. Come up at C; go in at D, diagonally across A-B; pull through. This forms raised, bumplike stitch.

under along the staystitching. Hemming may be unnecessary if you attach the appliqué with a tightly spaced machine zigzag stitch that solidly covers the raw edges.

For a puffy effect, tuck a bit of stuffing under the appliqué before you finish stitching it in place.

Batik. This ancient craft from Indonesia can turn a simple pillow toy into a work of art (see dolls on page 42). Batik, translated, means "wax writing." You dye fabric that has been partially coated with melted wax. The waxed areas retain the original color of the fabric (though fine lines may appear where the dye has seeped through cracks in the wax). After painting wax over the dyed portion of the fabric, you repeat the process with a second, and even a third color.

Use white or pastel fabric of natural fibers, prewashed to shrink it and to remove any sizing. Pure cotton pillowcases are just about right for toys. Choose permanent cold-water dyes in two or three colors that will blend harmoniously—the transparent dyes overlap, so if you use red and yellow, expect some orange in the finished design.

For soaking the fabric, you'll need a plastic or enamel dishpan. You'll also need either batik wax or equal parts of beeswax and paraffin (available at craft stores). To apply the melted wax, select a few natural-bristle brushes (these will be useless for anything else, so buy inexpensive ones). A special batik tool that works like a fountain pen may come in handy for drawing fine lines. It is called a *tjanting* (pronounced "chanting"); you can buy it at some art stores. You may also want to collect a few odds and ends to print with—wooden spools, a potato masher (wood or metal), a ball of string, or small wooden blocks.

Stretch your fabric quite flat using artist's stretcher bars—or tack it over an old picture frame. This raises the fabric so the wax can penetrate to the underside. Lightly pencil a design to follow as you apply the wax. Melt chunks of wax in cans placed in boiling water or in a double boiler. Be wary of wax—it is flammable. Never melt it directly over the heat source, and keep baking soda nearby to extinguish flames, just in case. (Water won't put them out.)

Melt the wax slowly. For good penetration, it should look translucent, not milky.

Check the dye packets for detailed instructions on dyeing. Immerse the cooled, waxed fabric in the palest color first. In successive dye baths, proceed gradually to the darkest shade, after applying wax over the paler dyes to keep them from discoloring. After each dye bath, rinse the fabric thoroughly and lay it flat to dry. Remove wax by ironing the fabric sandwiched between layers of paper towels. When your piece is finished, immerse it in boiling soapy water to remove any last traces of wax; then rinse thoroughly.

Putting it all together

Compared to most sewing projects, stitching up a toy goes very quickly.

The first step is to prepare your fabric by laundering it in the hottest water it can stand (if it is washable).

Press the fabric and straighten the grain (or weave), if necessary. The lengthwise grain is defined by the selvages. To find the crosswise grain, carefully pull a cross thread near one raw edge. If this line is perpendicular to the selvage, the fabric needs no straightening. If not, grasp opposite corners and pull along the bias, gradually working toward the center, until the weave is straight.

Cutting the cloth

Patterns are usually cut out in pairs—two or four pieces of fabric from one piece of paper. So fold your fabric in half, right sides together, following either the lengthwise or the crosswise grain.

Try to align the center of your pattern with the fabric grain. This is easy to do if you fold the pattern in half and rule a line along the fold mark. Keep this line either parallel or perpendicular to the selvages. If you're using a scrap without a selvage, study the weave and try to follow it.

Press pattern pieces smooth with a warm iron before pinning them in place.

If your fabric has a nap, be sure to lay all pattern pieces in the same direction. Before laying out patterns on fake fur, stroke the surface to find the direction of the nap. Just like the back of a dog, the fabric feels rough if you're pushing against the nap, smooth if you're stroking with it.

Sometimes the doubled cloth is too thick for scissors to cut. In this case, you'll have to pin and cut out the pattern from a single thickness twice (or for as many pairs as the pattern indicates). If it is an asymmetrical piece—like a mitten-shaped hand—turn the pattern face down

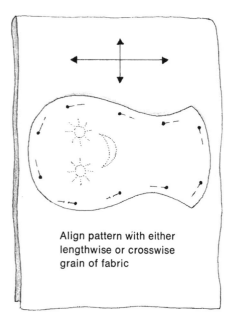

Align pattern with either lengthwise or crosswise grain of fabric

for the second cutting (and also for the fourth, if you need two pairs).

When cutting fake fur or extremely thick fabric, you may find a template easier to manage than a paper pattern. Just trace the pattern on cardboard, heavy plastic, or sandpaper (it grips the fabric), and cut out with scissors or a craft knife. With a soft lead pencil or tailor's chalk, trace the template on the wrong side of the fabric. If you need two or four pieces from one template, be sure to have the template face down the second and fourth times you trace it.

Try to avoid barbering fake fur when you cut it. Cut with the tips of your scissors, making sure that the lower blade is flat against the backing of the fur before you snip.

Before removing patterns from the cut-out cloth, transfer any guide marks that may be on them. To do this you may want to use one of the marking tools or kits sold at fabric shops for just this purpose. Usually the marks wash out unless you have ironed the fabric; check the product's instructions to be sure.

• Dressmaker's carbon paper is sold inexpensively in a kit with a tracing wheel. With the carbon side facing the fabric, lay a sheet of this paper between the fabric and the pattern—and a second sheet underneath if you're marking two pieces at once; then trace pattern marks with the tracing wheel.

• Fabric crayon pencils come with their own battery of colored tips. An easy way to use one is to push a pin through the pattern and the fabric, lift off the pattern, and mark at the pin point. If two pieces have been cut from one pattern, be sure to push the pin through both layers and to mark the underside as well as the top.

• Tailor's chalk is available in several colors as a flat cake or a pencil, and is used the same way as fabric crayon pencils.

Another transfer method that requires no special tools is simply to poke through the pattern with a sharpened soft lead pencil or a ballpoint pen, making tiny dots on the fabric. Accuracy is important here—especially if the fabric is pale —because the marks probably won't wash out.

If you cut out the pattern pieces carefully, you may not need to mark stitching lines except at tricky places such as tight curves. Instead, you might want to make a seam allowance guide for your sewing machine. Stick a short piece of masking tape down parallel to the line of stitching on the inside of the machine. Measure ¼ inch and ½ inch from the needle and rule parallel lines on the masking tape at these distances. As you sew, guide the outside edge of the fabric along one of these lines (for small toys a ¼-inch seam is usually enough).

Sewing for strength

Children's toys lead stressful lives—ears and tails get yanked, bodies are lovingly dragged across the floor by a foot or a handful of hair. Even if your creation is a soft sculpture destined for display on a shelf, strong stitching is important—stuffing strains seams, too.

To avoid minor but maddening tragedies—such as wavering seamlines or mismatched limbs—*baste* before your final stitching. To baste, take long running stitches by hand or machine (using the widest setting). Handbasting is especially helpful in neatly fitting a gusset such as the underbody of the animals on pages 46, 54, and 64. Basting is also the way to gather a seam—just pull the thread ends tight to pucker the cloth.

Before you begin sewing with your machine, make sure that both needle and thread correspond to the weight of your fabric. Thread is generally available in fine, medium, and heavy-duty weights. Needle sizes are numbered differently for different machines. Check your sewing machine manual or dealer if you're in doubt.

Use small, tightly spaced stitches. When sewing a tiny, curved piece—a foot or hand—stitch a second time over the first row of stitching so you can safely trim away most of the seam allowance. If you have the patience to stitch *everything* twice, the toy will be that much sturdier.

A good precaution (to prevent seams from ripping open during stuffing) is to make a few reverse stitches every three or four inches along seamlines.

When sewing by hand, use heavy-duty thread or dental floss. The slick surface of dental floss helps to ease it through fabric without tangling; it is extremely strong besides. Ordinary thread can also be slickened—just draw it through small pieces of soap, beeswax, or candle. For attaching yarn hair, you may prefer to use crochet twine in a matching color.

Two useful stitches for handsewing soft toys are shown at right. Use the cross-stitch for securing limbs, ears, and tails. The ladder stitch neatly laces up openings after the toy is stuffed.

Shaping up your toy

Rag dolls and teddy bears are boneless creatures. What gives them their shape is stuffing. Careful sewing counts, too, but it takes stuffing to transform a baggy heap of cloth into a toy. What you use for stuffing (see page 6) and how firmly you pack it will make a big difference in your finished project.

Most soft toys look better and last longer if you squeeze as much stuffing into them as you

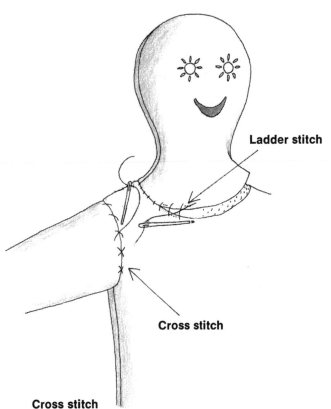

Cross stitch
Make row of diagonal stitches; stitching in reverse direction, cross first stitches with second row

Ladder stitch
Make three small running stitches on one side of opening; cross to other side and take three more; pull thread tight to lace up opening

can. Strategic places, such as a doll's neck or the tops of an animal's legs, need to be very solidly packed or they will become wobbly. (You might even want to put a short piece of dowel in the center of the neck and upper body.)

Binding the opening of your toy with masking tape helps to keep the raw edges from fraying as you work.

Stuff a little at a time. If you're using polyester fiber or some similar fluffy substance, wrap a bit of it on the end of a stick—a wooden chopstick or dowel—and use the stick to poke the stuffing into corners and to pack it firmly. (A crochet hook is handy for reaching tiny places like thumbs.) Test with your fingers—if you can dent the stuffing, you can add still more.

Though it takes extra time, it is a good idea to let a fully stuffed toy settle overnight before you sew it closed. The next day you'll probably find you can pack it even fuller.

Making faces

Many people feel unsure when it comes to putting a face on a doll or an animal. But faces don't have to be fussy or difficult. Even the simplest hint of personality — a pair of button eyes or three dots of embroidery — can be surprisingly expressive. It is easy to overcrowd a small face. Besides, there's really no need to aim for flawless beauty. Raggedy Ann and Andy are all the more lovable for their foolish grins.

Consider your toy's character and the kind of expression you'd like to achieve. The sketches below give you some ideas. Children's book illustrations are another good source of inspiration.

Some useful techniques for rendering faces are described on page 9. Take time to doodle on scraps of paper and to experiment. Before stitching on buttons or appliqués, shift them around on the doll's face until they form just the right expression.

By pulling the thread very taut as you stitch button eyes, you can contour the face slightly (at the same time anchoring the eyes firmly in place). For added realism and humor, you might prefer plastic eyes with loose rolling pupils (sold at craft stores).

Face ideas

Plastic eyes with rolling pupils; chain-stitched nose and mouth

Felt eyes with wood button pupils; French knots around nose; satin-stitched nose and chain-stitched mouth (see page 39)

Felt or iron-on patch appliqué (see page 24)

Felt eyes and mouth; lashes drawn with felt-tip pen (see page 27)

Stitches taken under stuffing to bulge cheeks; satin-stitched eyes and nose; outline-stitched mouth (see page 49)

Button nose, pupils; other features are appliquéd felt

Velvet covered button eyes; stuffed felt appliqué nose; chain-stitched mouth (see page 62)

Outline or split-stitched features with satin stitches covering solid areas of eyes, cheeks (see page 22)

On a doll you can knot the thread at the back of the head where it will later be covered with hair. You'll need to use a very long needle; an upholstery needle may be necessary for a large doll. Stitch through to the front of the head, catching the button, and back again — several times. Pull the stitches very tight until the button presses against the stuffing, creating a shallow indentation around the eye. If you don't want stitching to show on the back of the head, you can create the same tension by sewing between two button eyes, using a curved upholstery needle.

Another way to model the face is to topstitch with a small needle and fine thread or a few strands of embroidery floss. The toy should be fully stuffed, but not yet sewn closed. To make a round nose or fleshy cheeks, use a crochet hook to poke a bit of stuffing in position, just under the fabric. Take tiny stitches around the plumped-up area, and several stitches underneath, to hold it in place.

Wigs, manes, and tails

There is a wealth of fur, fluff, and fuzz in the world just waiting to coif your toy. Browse through yarn and craft stores to collect ideas, or visit specialty shops that supply materials for macramé and weaving. Here is just a taste of what you'll find:
• Thick rug yarn — tidy and durable, excellent for a pony's or a lion's mane.
• Fluffy mohair yarn — fine, curly, and brushable.
• Tapestry yarn — available in small bundles in a gorgeous array of colors.
• Unspun wool — straight from the sheep, beautiful, earthy, and quite realistic.
• Woven nylon cord — unravel the threads to produce tight curls.
• Gift wrap yarn — brush it to make it billowy.
• Camel's hair — available as a package of warm brown fluff.

Also check theatrical suppliers and thrift shops for synthetic, human-scale wigs, switches, and beards — and fabric shops for fringe.

Sometimes just a small wad of yarn or fluff, shaped on the head and stitched in place, creates an elegant hairdo. Fine hair goes on more easily if you stitch it to a bit of seam binding, and then sew the seam binding to the head. Thick hair of rug yarn can be sewn in place strand by strand. You can also fashion a wig, mane, or tail in the style of a mop, as shown at the right. Make looped curls almost the same way. Wrap the yarn around something long and narrow, like a ruler. Sew up one side and slip the ruler out. Attach the sewn side to the doll's head.

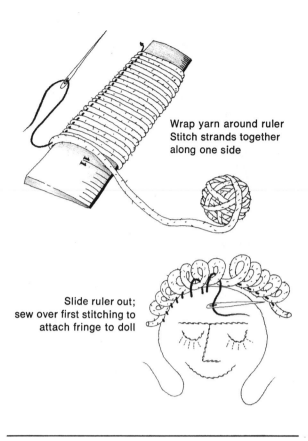

Wrap yarn around ruler
Stitch strands together along one side

Slide ruler out; sew over first stitching to attach fringe to doll

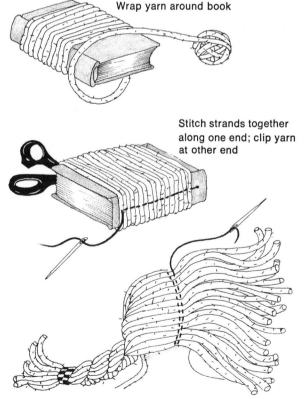

Wrap yarn around book

Stitch strands together along one end; clip yarn at other end

Sew to doll over first stitching, making center part

Our doll potpourri

The ancestry of dolls is probably about as far-flung as our own. It seems that people have always needed dolls — for comfort, for worship, for learning, or simply for celebration of the human experience.

In this chapter we introduce you to a few members of today's generation of dolls. Some are obviously meant for children. Others will win the hearts of more mature doll lovers as well. And a few could be aptly described as soft sculptures. On the next 29 pages you'll find 41 different doll characters you can make.

Appliqué gingerbread man

Looking good enough to eat, our gingerbread boy is a livewire like his cousin in the story (the cooky that jumped out of the old woman's oven and ran away). Have fun decorating him. Take a holiday from your conscience and lavish him with "sugar"—fabric frosting, rickrack licorice, shiny button gumdrops. When he's done, present him to a lucky child (or if he looks too delicious to give away, sit him on your sofa instead). Our cooky—see photo, opposite—was designed by Carole Austin.

You'll need: 1 yard 60-inch-wide ginger-colored velour (or 2 yards 45-inch-wide corduroy); felt squares (we used 3 pink, 2 mustard, 1 orange); 1 package *each* wide and medium-size rickrack; white yarn; turquoise embroidery floss; 3 buttons for chest; 2 large white buttons for eyes; 1 small white button for nose; 2 bags polyester stuffing.

Putting him together

1) Enlarge and transfer pattern (facing page) for doll. Cut front and back from velour or corduroy (doubled, right sides together). Draw your own appliqués or trace those shown on our pattern. Cut these from felt squares. Mark right side of of 1 velour piece (doll front) for placement of appliqués and rickrack (see page 12 for transfer methods).

2) Pin appliqués in position. Secure with zigzag or straight machine stitches. Pin and stitch down rickrack, using wide size for mouth.

3) Sew buttons in place for eyes, nose, and chest trimming.

4) With white yarn, take straight stitches for lashes and flower petals. Make French knots (see page 11) to dot lashes, decorate rickrack, make flower centers. With turquoise floss, outline hearts and add any further trimming desired.

5) With right sides facing, stitch doll front to back, making ½" seam, leaving 6" open in 1 leg. Clip curves, turn right side out, and stuff. Blindstitch opening closed.

Variation: Without enlarging our pattern, make a dozen gingerbread cookies of multicolored patchwork. Present in a basket to a small child.

OUT OF THE OVEN, into your arms. See facing page for directions on how to make a piping hot gingerbread man of your own.

Gingerbread man: Enlarge on 1″ grid • ½″ seam allowance

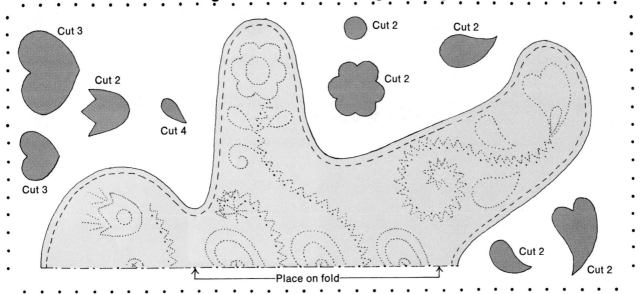

Cut 3

Cut 2

Cut 3

Cut 4

Cut 2

Cut 2

Cut 2

Cut 2

Cut 2

←—Place on fold—→

(See "Pattern transfer" on page 6)

Dolls: Gingerbread man **17**

Each of these chubby cherubs is a reorganized baby sock. Simple enough for children to sew, the dolls have embroidered details that will delight experienced stitchers as well. To mention just a few possibilities—you might give one sock baby a tattoo, another a string of pearls, a belly-button, or a polka dot necktie. The sock babies on the facing page (upper photo) were designed by Joice Beatty.

You'll need: For *each* doll—a child's cotton sock, size 4 to 6; white thread; embroidery floss; polyester stuffing; fabric scraps for clothing, if desired.

Putting them together

1) Cut off sock toe just inside printed size coding. Turn sock inside out; stitch to outline legs as shown in sketch 1. Clip between legs; trim seam. Turn right side out and stuff to cuff ribbing.

2) Following sketch 2, tie sock at lower edge of ribbing to form neck. Stuff ribbing; gather closed 1 or 2" from scalloped top edge. Fold this edge over head, forming cap; blindstitch in place.

3) Cut printed coding off sock toe. Turn inside out; mark center with pin (see sketch 3). Stitch 2 seams parallel to pin. Cut between them, creating 2 arms. Turn right side out, stuff, stitch closed, and attach to doll.

4) Embroider faces and details with bright floss (see page 10 for sketches of useful stitches).

5) To make dress, cut rectangle of fabric twice as wide as doll and twice as long plus 1". Fold in half and cut large head hole in center of fold (see sketch 4). With right sides together, stitch side seams, leaving ¾" open for armholes. Hem neckline, armholes, and lower edge of dress. Gather neckline with embroidery floss, leaving 2 lengths free at center to draw up and tie after putting dress on doll.

Sock babies

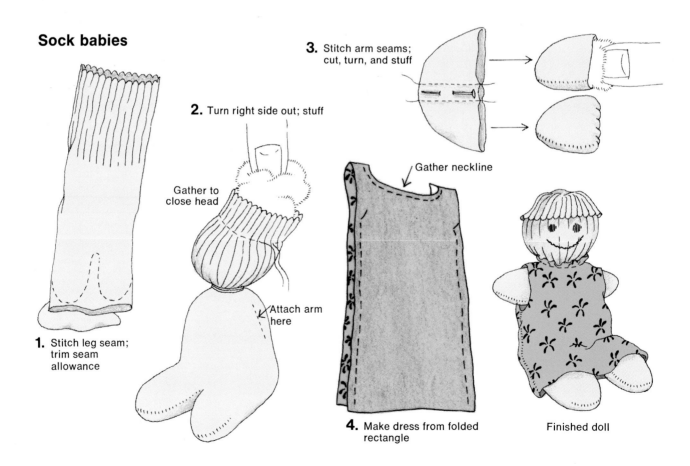

3. Stitch arm seams; cut, turn, and stuff

2. Turn right side out; stuff

Gather to close head

Attach arm here

1. Stitch leg seam; trim seam allowance

Gather neckline

4. Make dress from folded rectangle

Finished doll

"ROCKABYE, SOCK BABIES, in the treetop . . ."
You make these plump little dolls from baby socks
(see opposite page).

Pipe cleaner people

Bring a doll house to life with a happy little family of pipe cleaner people. You can make a crowd of these charming Lilliputians with a few pipe cleaners, shoe strings, and sewing scraps.

These lithe little people fit comfortably into miniature chairs, beds, and cars. Crook one pipe cleaner "hand," and they can safely hold a tiny china teacup. Our family (see doll house below) was designed by Marlene Heinz.

You'll need: For *each* doll (tallest is 6 inches)— 2 pipe cleaners; 1 shoelace or 12 inches of hollow cording; scrap of flesh-colored stretch fabric, such as nylon tricot, for face; fabric scraps for

PIPE CLEANER PEOPLE invite mother and daughter to share the pleasure of doll play.

clothing; lace for trimming; knitted glove for cap and sweater; felt scraps for shoes; yarn scraps for hair; tiny beads for eyes; small amount polyester stuffing; white thread; red embroidery floss.

Putting them together

1) Form body by twisting 2 pipe cleaners together, following sketches below. With pipe cleaners lined up evenly, twist to create torso, starting 3″ from 1 end. Continue twisting until torso is 2″ long; then twist backwards for ¾″, overlapping last twists of torso. This creates neck. Ends of pipe cleaners now resemble arms and legs; bend them out to each side.

2) To make head, cut out 3″ diameter circle (baby's is 1½″ circle) of stretch fabric. Hand-baste around perimeter of circle. Put heaping tablespoonful stuffing into center; pull basting thread to gather circle tightly around stuffing. Fit neck into head opening. Stitch head securely around neck, taking several stitches under each arm as well.

3) If doll is a child, trim arms and legs (untwist torso once or twice to shorten it before trimming legs). Cut shoelace to match arm and leg lengths of doll, adding ½″ to each. Thread onto pipe cleaners; tuck raw edges inside and stitch closed at hands (shoes will cover feet).

4) To make dress, cut fabric scraps as follows: two 2″ squares for sleeves, one 2½ by 3″ rectangle for bodice, and one 4 by 6″ rectangle for skirt. (For child, cut pieces to fit after measuring doll.) Hem both longer sides of bodice and skirt and 2 opposite sides of each sleeve. With right sides together, seam raw edges of each piece, making tubes.

5) Turn tubes right side out; put bodice and sleeves on doll (slip feet through bodice) with seams at back of bodice and at underarms of sleeves. Blindstitch sleeves and neck edge to head, taking tucks as necessary. Cover stitches with lace or other trim. Stuff polyester stuffing through cuff and waist openings (tweezers help here). Gather edges of openings tightly to close around hands and waist. Gather 1 edge of skirt tube, slip on doll, pull gathers tight, and blindstitch to waist.

6) Make man's shirt as you did bodice in step 5, adding necktie instead of lace. Cut two 2½ by 3″ rectangles of fabric for pants. Hem 2½″ sides of each. Place right sides together and seam both 3″ sides. Stitch inner leg seam at center, 1¾″ up from 1 hemmed edge. Clip between legs, trim seams, and turn right side out. Put on doll, make tucks in back to fit waist, and stitch in place.

7) To make sweater, cut finger of knitted glove into torso-length tube and 2 arm-length rectangles. Finish as you did bodice in step 5. Cut off fingertip of glove for hat. Hem raw edge and turn back for brim.

8) Make shoes of black felt: Stitch together 2 U-shaped pieces for each shoe after tracing doll's foot. Turn right side out, slip on foot, and stitch to shoestring that covers leg.

9) Make faces. We used tiny beads for eyes, a few stitches with red embroidery floss for mouths. To make round noses: Knot white thread at back of head; pass needle through stuffing and bring up at center of face. Stitch back and forth, passing needle under stuffing, working gradually in a circle; pull stitches tight to make nose bulge. Sew on scraps of yarn for hair.

Pipe cleaner people

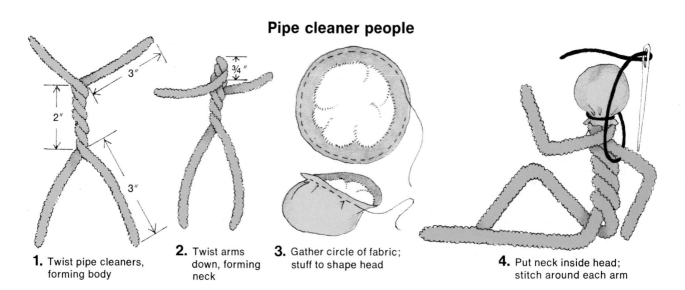

1. Twist pipe cleaners, forming body

2. Twist arms down, forming neck

3. Gather circle of fabric; stuff to shape head

4. Put neck inside head; stitch around each arm

Waking/sleeping dolls

(Photos on pages 22 and 80)

Children will love these cuddly, round-the-clock companions. On one side, they're wide awake and full of fun, ready for hours of play. But turn them over—suddenly they're fast asleep in cozy pajamas, gently coaxing their young owners to bed.

The boys and girls on the next page were designed by M. Geri Tanji Carey.

You'll need: For *each* 14-inch doll — ½ yard of 45-inch-wide muslin or similar flesh-tone fabric; fabric scraps for clothing; snaps or buttons for boy's pajamas; 1 yard ¼-inch-wide bias tape for girl's nightgown; yarn scraps for hair; embroidery floss for facial features; ½ bag polyester stuffing.

Boy doll

1) Enlarge and transfer pattern (page 23), following outline for boy. To make daytime clothing patterns, trace outlines for pants and shirt, adding ½" to each at waist. Trace doll pattern for pajama appliqué. Cut out doll front and back from doubled fabric. Cut clothing from single layers of fabric scraps.

2) Press under raw edges of shirt neckline and sleeves ¼". Pin shirt to doll front. Baste close to edge along arms and sides; topstitch at sleeves and neckline.

3) Press under ½" along bottom and waist edges of pants. Topstitch pocket outline or appliqué real pocket. Hem 2 straps or suspenders, if desired, each 4½" by 1". Pin pants and straps in place, overlapping shirt. Baste along sides; topstitch at waist and cuffs; tack straps to shoulders.

4) Press under pajama neck edge ¼". Topstitch details such as waistline, front placket. Sew on buttons or snaps. Pin pajamas to doll back; baste all around and topstitch neckline.

5) Stitch ear fronts to backs, right sides together, making ⅛" seams. Stitch again to reinforce.

Turn, stuff, and baste to doll front with outer edge of each ear turned toward face.

6) Pin doll front to doll back, right sides together. With front facing you, stitch ½" seam all around, leaving 3" opening in 1 side. Take care to stitch just outside pants stitching at cuff. Stitch curve between legs extending above pants stitching. Trim seam, clip curves and corners, and turn right side out. Stuff; stitch closed.

7) Use light pencil or fabric crayon to draw face details — eyes open on 1 side, closed on other side. Embroider lines with outline stitch, solid areas with satin stitch. Make French knots for curly hair, long running stitches with loose ends for straight hair (see page 10 on embroidery). Style thick hair with few lengths of yarn sewn to center and sides of head.

Girl doll

1) Enlarge and transfer pattern (page 23), following outline for girl. Trace doll for daytime dress pattern. Trace nightgown pattern. Cut out girl doll and clothing same as for boy (see step 1).

2) Appliqué heart to dress (see page 10). Finish neckline with appliquéd collar, lace, or bias tape. Lay dress in position on doll front; at outside of each leg, clip lower edge ½". Press under hem between clips; reopen hem. Pin crease of hem to doll front, right sides together, as shown on page 22. Stitch along crease, attaching dress to doll front.

3) Lay dress over doll front. Baste close to edge along sides and arms.

4) Make 2" slit in nightgown at center of neckline. With bias tape, first bind slit, then neckline, leaving 4" lengths free to tie. Pin nightgown to doll back and baste close to edge.

5) Finish by following steps 6 and 7 for boy (preceding), omitting curve between legs.

AWAKE OR ASLEEP, any one of these boy and girl dolls could become someone's best friend. Directions start on page 21.

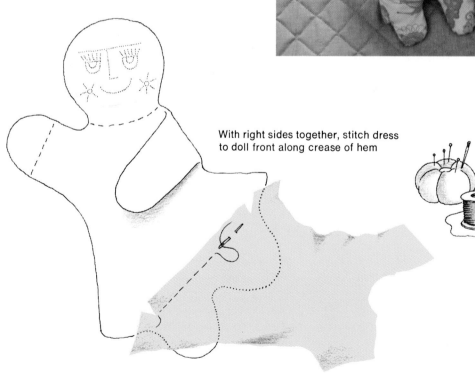

With right sides together, stitch dress to doll front along crease of hem

Waking/sleeping doll: Enlarge on 1″ grid ● ½″ seam allowance

(See "Pattern transfer" on page 6)

Nightgown appliqué—
cut 1

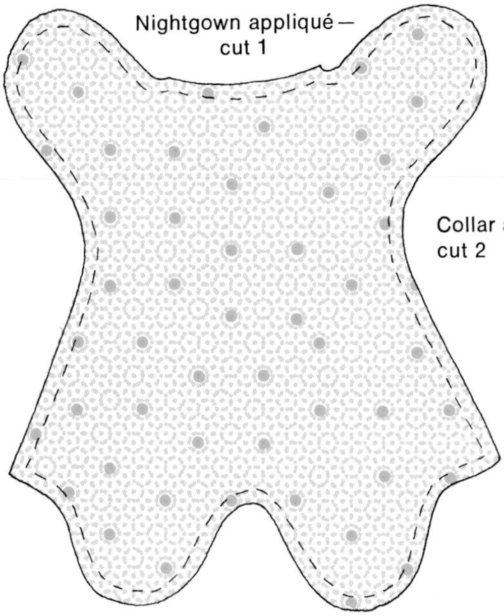

Girl front & back—
cut 2

Collar appliqué—
cut 2

Dress appliqué—
cut 1

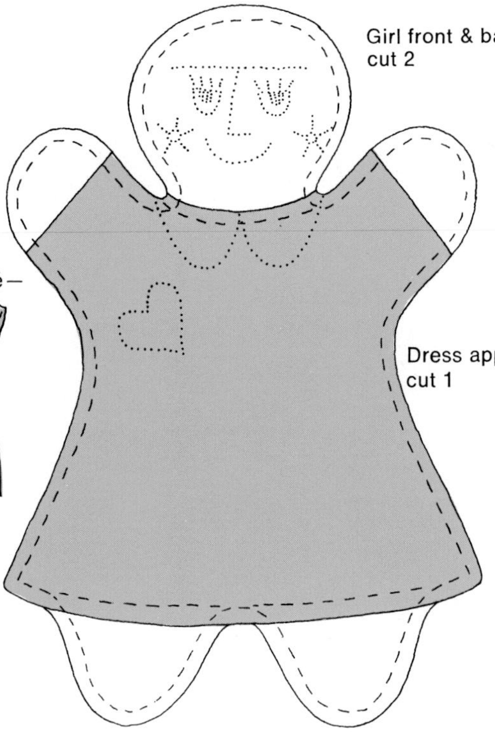

Boy front & back—
cut 2

Pants & shirt appliqué—cut 1 each

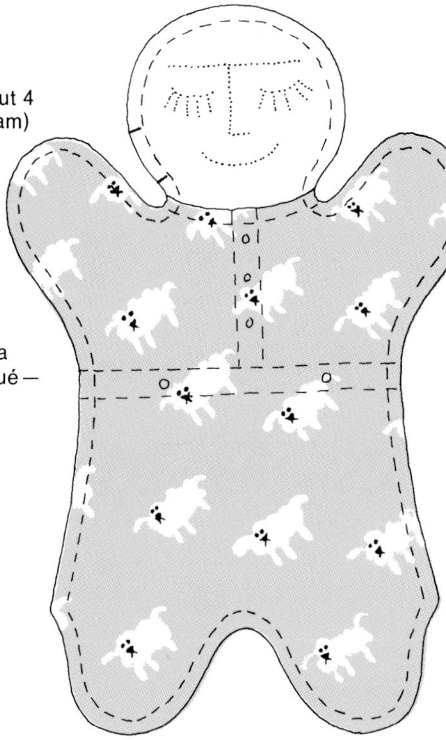

Ears—cut 4
(⅛″ seam)

Pajama
appliqué—
cut 1

Add ½″ seam
allowance at waist
to pants & shirt

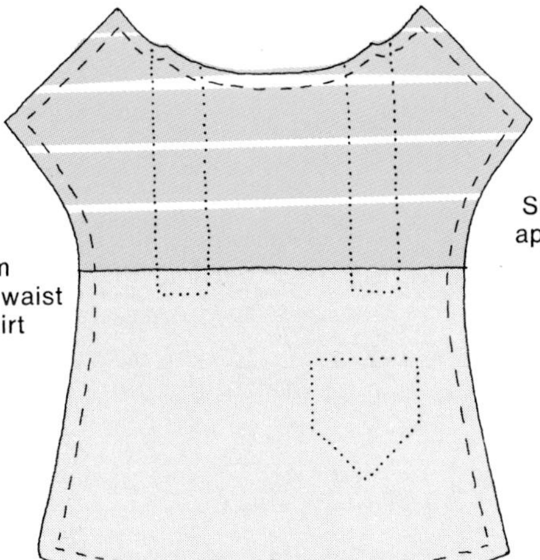

Suspender
appliqués—
cut 2

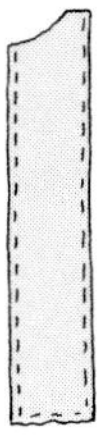

Pocket—cut 1

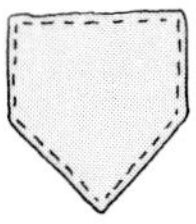

Louis Looselimbs

COME ON, LOUIS, let's shake a leg . . . let's polka, jig, and boogaloo.

Hair flying and limbs flapping, Louis kicks, twists, hops—even tangos and polkas. He's got rhythm, he's got music. All he needs is a partner.

Standing on his own two feet, Louis is not terribly well coordinated. But elastic bands sewn to his toes slip over his partner's feet to help guide his wobbly steps. You can further his antics by adding snap tabs to clasp his hands and feet together in a wild Russian leap, or to encircle his arms around your neck. He was designed by Kathy Brenzel.

You'll need: For a 4-foot dancing partner — 2 yards of 45-inch-wide sturdy cotton (sailcloth, duck, or similar fabric); ⅓ yard plain fabric for face; felt scraps for features; yarn scraps for hair; ⅓ yard elastic for foot loops; 4 heavy-duty snap fasteners for tabs (available in a kit with tool for attaching them); 2 bags polyester stuffing.

Putting him together

1) Enlarge and transfer pattern (opposite page) to heavy paper. Trace face pattern on separate sheet. Fold fabric lengthwise, right sides together, allowing 6½" of bottom layer to extend beyond top layer (see sketch 1). Cut out doll front. Fold remaining fabric again lengthwise. Place pattern in reverse at opposite end (see sketch 2).

Fold excess fabric near head, right sides together, under arm, extending ½" for seam allowance where right arm is pieced to doll back. Cut out doll back. Trim top side of body where arm will join, leaving ½" seam allowance. Join arm to body.

2) Cut face from plain fabric. Press under ¼" along bottom edge. Matching raw edges of face and doll front, appliqué face to doll along pressed edge. Baste ¼" from edge along sides and top of head. Arrange felt features and stitch in place.

3) To make snap tabs, cut four 2" squares of fabric. Fold each in half, right sides together. Stitch ¼" from edge across 1 end and down side, leaving other end open. Turn right side out; press. Attach snaps to each pair of tabs near closed ends, following kit directions.

4) Matching open edges of tabs with edges of hands and toes, baste tabs to right side of doll front, ¼" from edge. Cut 2 pieces of elastic long enough to loop comfortably around child's foot. Baste ends of each loop near tabs to right side of toes.

5) After making sure tabs and loops are tucked inside, join doll front to back, right sides together, making ½" seam. Leave head open between notches. Turn right side out; stuff.

6) Cut equal lengths of yarn for hair. Arrange inside head opening. Tuck under raw edges and stitch opening closed, adding stuffing as you go.

Variation: Give Louis a top hat and tails, like Fred Astaire.

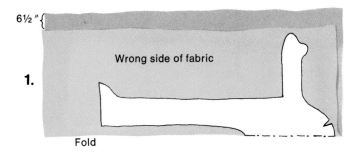

6½"

1.

Wrong side of fabric

Fold

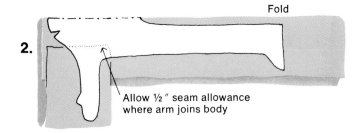

Fold

2.

Allow ½" seam allowance where arm joins body

Louis Looselimbs:

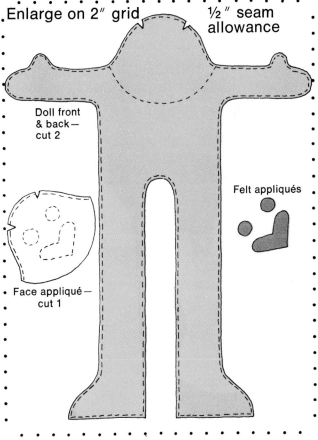

Enlarge on 2" grid ½" seam allowance

Doll front & back— cut 2

Face appliqué— cut 1

Felt appliqués

(See "Pattern transfer" on page 6)

Dolls: Louis Looselimbs **25**

Goldibraids – a doll with dresses

Goldibraids, with a miniature trunk full of dresses, would entrance any little girl on Christmas morning.

Technically she is a rag doll, modeled after forebears that were carefully stitched by hand a century ago. Our modern Goldibraids is made of muslin as they were — but her only rags are glad ones.

You'll need: For doll — ½ yard 45-inch-wide muslin (for darker skin tone, dye in coffee or tea); for *each* dress, nightgown, or set of undergarments — ½ yard lightweight cotton or cotton blend fabric; 1 black felt square for boots; felt scraps or embroidery floss for features; 2-ounce skein bulky yarn for braids (or mohair for curls); ½ yard of ¼-inch elastic cord; 1 yard eyelet, lace, or other trimming; thread to match fabrics used for doll and dresses; dental floss; crochet twine to match hair color; snaps or self-gripping tape; 1 bag polyester stuffing.

Putting her together

1) Enlarge and transfer doll patterns below. Cut out from muslin (folded lengthwise). Do same with patterns for clothing (page 29), cutting garments from fabrics folded lengthwise, right sides facing. Transfer pattern marks to fabrics. Trace lower leg pattern to make boot pattern, adding ½" all around. Cut 4 pieces from black felt.

2) Pin together front and back pieces for arms, legs, head, and torso. Making ¼" seams, stitch arms and legs along sides and curves of hands and feet. Stitch hand and foot seams over 1st stitching for reinforcement. Stitch head front to head back, leaving neck open. Stitch together front and back of torso at sides (A to B) and shoulders (C to D).

3) Clip curves and turn pieces right side out. (To ease turning long arms and legs, nudge dowel

Goldibraids: Enlarge on 1″ grid • ¼″ seam allowance (See "Pattern transfer" on page 6)

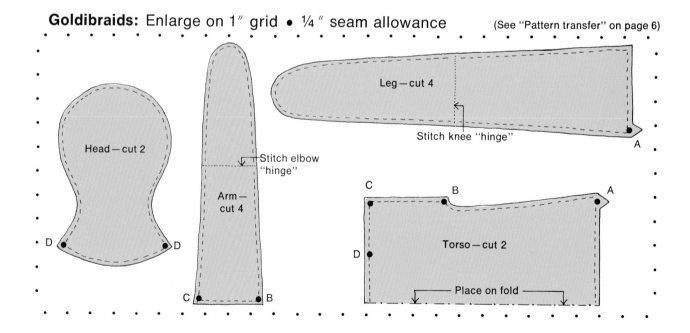

Head—cut 2

Arm—cut 4

Stitch elbow "hinge"

Leg—cut 4

Stitch knee "hinge"

Torso—cut 2

Place on fold

GOLDIBRAIDS, a classic rag doll, sits munching lunch and wishing a few bears would join her.

into hand or toe area and, with dowel held upright in 1 hand, slide arm or leg tube down over it. Tube turns right side out as you pull.)

4) Stuff extremities of arms and legs, using dowel to pack firmly. Stop where knees and elbows are indicated on pattern (5″ from hands, 8″ from feet). Using zipper foot, stitch across (perpendicular to seam), creating "hinges." Lightly stuff upper portions of limbs.

5) Press under raw edges of armholes ½″. Place open ends of arms inside armholes. Using zip-

per foot, stitch from B to C. Press under bottom edges of torso ½″. Place open ends of legs inside near hips; stitch between notches as you stitched armholes.

6) Stuff torso firmly through center opening in shoulder seam. Stuff head and neck. Turn under raw edge of neck and pin over shoulders. Hand-stitch securely in place with dental floss, adding stuffing up to last stitch to keep neck firm.

7) To make braids (see sketches on next page), wrap yarn thickly around book or board (size determines hair length). At 1 end, stitch rows of yarn together with matching crochet twine, making 5"-long seam (bunch yarn as you sew). Cut other end of yarn, slip off book, and sew over previous stitching to center of doll's head. Braid each side. Stitch yarn to head just above braids. Make face using glued felt scraps, embroidery stitches, or both (see page 14 for ideas).

8) With right sides together, stitch dress or nightgown bodice fronts to backs at shoulders. Cut bodice back down center, neck to waist. Make ½" casing in 1 long side of each sleeve, leaving 1" unstitched for insertion of elastic cord. Gather remaining long side of each sleeve.

9) With right sides together, pull sleeve gathers to fit armholes of bodice. Pin and stitch armhole seams. Stitch side and sleeve seams, stopping at casings. Insert elastic cord 4" long in casings at sleeve cuffs; stitch ends together and close casings.

10) With right sides together, stitch side seams of skirt, D to E. Slit and hem center back, 3" from waist. Gather waist, starting and stopping 1" from back opening. With right sides together, stitch gathered skirt waist to bodice waist, matching back openings. Hem skirt and raw edges of bodice. Trim neckline with lace. Sew snaps or self-gripping tape to back opening.

11) Pin bloomer pieces right sides together, and stitch center front and back seams (A to B). Press seams open. Hem waist edge ½", leaving 1" open for insertion of elastic cord. Trim cuffs with eyelet; then stitch inner leg seam (C to B to C). Insert 17" of elastic cord into casing at waist; stitch ends together and close casing.

12) Make petticoat like skirt, treating waist like waist of bloomers. Trim with eyelet.

13) Stitch together 2 U-shaped pieces for each boot, making ⅛" seams. Turn so that seams are inside. Slip boots on doll.

Goldibraids' wig

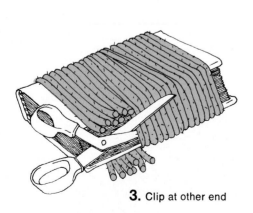

1. Wrap yarn around book

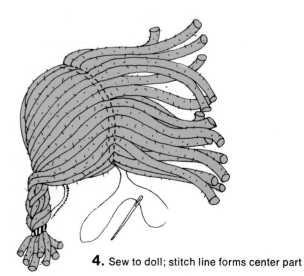

2. Stitch along one end

3. Clip at other end

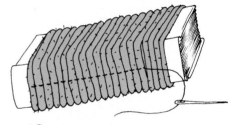

4. Sew to doll; stitch line forms center part

Clothing variations

Goldibraids' clothing: Enlarge on 1″ grid • ¼″ seam allowance

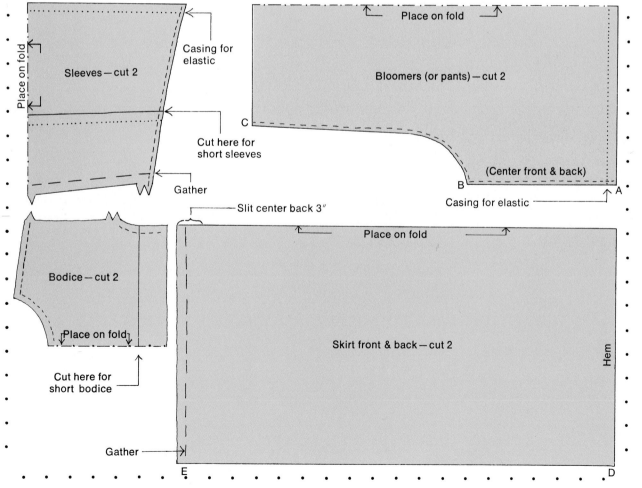

Place on fold

Sleeves — cut 2

Casing for elastic

Cut here for short sleeves

Gather

Place on fold

Bloomers (or pants) — cut 2

C

B ⌐ A

(Center front & back)

Casing for elastic

Bodice — cut 2

Place on fold

Cut here for short bodice

Slit center back 3″

Place on fold

Skirt front & back — cut 2

Hem

Gather

E

D

(See "Pattern transfer" on page 6)

*MA AND PA PILLOW **(above)** and Child
Pillow **(left)** pose softly for their portraits.*

Pillow portraits

You trace a real person to determine size and shape; then you stitch up a cozy pillow person (call it a soft "portrait"). Sit him in an extra rocker or lounge her on a wicker day bed. Arrange one against a wall to curl up on while watching T V Try dressing your pillow in a costume or, if it is child-size, in outgrown clothing. One woman we know sent a pillow person to a party she couldn't attend.

Decorating the portait depends on your personal taste and inclination. We machine embroidered the muslin couple on the facing page. If you want to keep your portrait simpler, like our Child Pillow, just sew on button eyes and fluff for hair. All three of these dolls are the work of Karen Cummings.

You might also try fabric paints (available at art supply stores) for splashy colors. Other decorative techniques are discussed on page 9.

You'll need: For adult size — 5 yards of preshrunk 60-inch-wide muslin (which can be dyed in coffee or tea); for child size — 4 yards of muslin or other skin-tone fabric. Also thread to match as well as to contrast brightly for machine embroidery; buttons for eyes and sheep's wool or yarn for hair, if not embroidered; 4 to 6 bags polyester stuffing (or foam chips for squishy pillow).

Putting them together

1) After pressing fabric to make as smooth as possible, fold in half, right sides together. Spread on clean floor. Have subject lie on fabric with arms slightly spread. With pencil or chalk, lightly trace all around, several inches away from body. (Subject may now get up off hard floor.)

2) Pin fabric layers together inside pencil outline, and cut out, staying ½" *outside* line.

3) To make dolls in style of muslin couple (facing page), machine embroider details of face, hair,

fingers, and clothing on pillow front. If this technique is new to you, experiment first on fabric scraps and see page 9. You don't necessarily need a zigzag machine, though it produces thicker lines. Loosen presser foot or remove it. Adjust thread tension until you achieve effect you like. Just guide fabric under needle and "draw." For fairly precise details, such as eyes, you may want to follow light pencil guidelines.

4) When front of pillow is finished, pin front to back, right sides together. Stitch all around, making ½" seam, leaving 8" open in 1 leg. Clip angles and curves; turn right side out. Stuff with polyester stuffing or fill with foam chips poured through large funnel (see page 6 for coping with mess). Stitch opening closed.

5) If you like, you might quilt portions of pillow, such as tops of legs (so it can sit easily) or fingers (to delineate).

6) For doll in style of our Child Portrait (facing page), sew on eyes and sheep's wool hair.

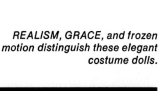

REALISM, GRACE, and frozen motion distinguish these elegant costume dolls.

Ballet troupe of bendable dolls

Like putty in your hands, these dolls bend into almost any conceivable position. The secret of their supple grace is a wire skeleton. Fattened with batting and costumed, they become dancers, acrobats, gymnasts — or any other limber character that sparks your fancy.

Our dolls, designed by Francoise Kirkman, re-create ballet poses from *Swan Lake*. If you would like to simulate your own favorite ballet instead, save your ballet program for ideas. Illustrated books from the library are also good sources for both dance and costume ideas.

Note: These dolls are for display rather than for active play. It is best to stop bending them once you've found the perfect pose — eventually the wire will snap. Also, if your hands are not strong, you may need help in twisting the wire.

You'll need: For *each* 14-inch doll — 72 inches of 14-gauge wire; small skein of white yarn; fabric scraps including skin-tone knit fabric and felt; trimmings such as lace, dime store jewelry, craft store feathers, flowers from old hats; fluff for hair (see page 15 for ideas); white glue; felt-tip pens or embroidery floss for facial features; polyester stuffing or quilt batting; 1½-inch-wide dowel (any length) or wooden handle of similar width and shape; wire cutters; 2 pairs of pliers.

Putting it together

1) For *each* doll, cut 2 lengths of wire — one 29", one 48". As shown in sketch 1 at right, place centers together and bend both around dowel. Using 1 pair of pliers to grip wire and the other pair to twist, form loop around dowel by twisting several times underneath. Make twisted wire about ¾" long to form neck.

2) Bend 2 shorter lengths horizontally for arms. Bend each arm in half, twisting several times toward shoulder. Leave loops for hands.

3) Twist 2 longer pieces for 4", creating torso. Separate legs, treating them as you did arms, with loops for feet (see sketch 2).

4) Wrap wads of stuffing or squares of batting around wire, binding them with yarn, as shown in sketch 3. Continue until body is shapely. Bind neck tightly with yarn.

5) Push small handful of stuffing into head loop (see sketch 4). Bind well with yarn to cover both stuffing and wire. Cut 4″ circle of knit fabric. Place center over face. Trim neck as shown in sketch 5. Gather edge of circle and pull tight, adding stuffing to fill out face. Stitch at back of head, pulling fabric to make it smooth in front. Stitch back of neck, pulling under chin to prevent wrinkling.

6) Cover hands and/or arms (if no sleeves) with felt strips long enough to cover arms and wide enough to wrap underneath. Pin to fit snugly. Snip where necessary, and stitch.

7) Make dress or doublet from 12″ circle of fabric as described on page 9. Gather long rectangle for skirt. To make fitted bodice, measure torso and pin felt rectangles larger than measurement to front and back. Carefully snip, pin, and stitch to fit. Add trimming (we used dime store bracelet for man's belt, pin in ballerina's hair).

8) Make felt tights as you did arms and hands, or use knitted gloves or socks. Hold doll over knitted material and trace, adding seam allowance. Cut out and pin to doll. Stitch, tucking in raw edges at back and pulling tight for neat fit.

9) Ballet slippers are made of 2″ felt circles. As shown in sketch 6, cut oval out of center. Slip foot into oval opening; stitch around rim. Fold and stitch perimeter of circle to bottom of foot. Sew on sole of felt.

10) See page 15 for hairstyle ideas (remember to cover stitching at back of head). See page 14 for face ideas (we sketched simple features with felt-tip pens).

Bendable dolls

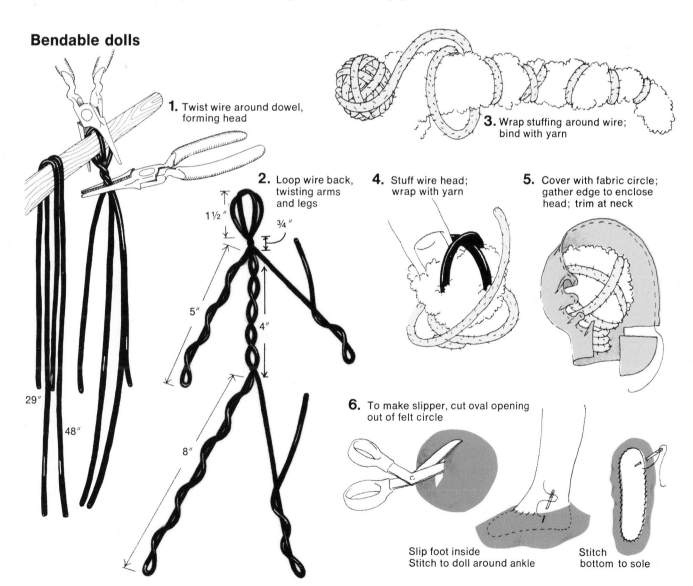

1. Twist wire around dowel, forming head

2. Loop wire back, twisting arms and legs

1½″   ¾″   5″   4″   8″   29″   48″

3. Wrap stuffing around wire; bind with yarn

4. Stuff wire head; wrap with yarn

5. Cover with fabric circle; gather edge to enclose head; trim at neck

6. To make slipper, cut oval opening out of felt circle

Slip foot inside
Stitch to doll around ankle

Stitch bottom to sole

Matryoshka— a mama and babies

Matryoshka (pronounced "Matrushka") and her children are patchwork renditions of traditional Russian nesting dolls. In Russia, the wooden figures celebrate fertility, the Mama doll concealing as many as 70 children in her hollow interior.

The Mama on the facing page carries her babies in pockets, kangaroo-style. Though her designer, Martie Sandell, gave her only two, you could give your own doll a larger family by adding pockets or tucking several children in each one.

You'll need: For a 14-inch Mama with 7-inch and 3½-inch children — assorted fabric scraps or printed cotton in 3 colors (two ¼-yard pieces and one ½-yard piece); scraps of muslin or other flesh-tone fabric for faces; ribbon, lace, or other trimming; thread to match fabrics and trimming; embroidery floss for hair and facial features; 1½ bags polyester stuffing.

Putting them together

1) Enlarge and transfer patterns (page 36). After selecting pleasing fabric combinations, cut out babushka, body, and pocket pieces. Cut faces (below) from muslin or other fabric.

2) With right sides facing, pair and pin together pocket pieces. Stitch each pair, leaving 3 inches open in one straight side (all seams are ¼"). Clip curves, turn right side out, and press. Stitch openings closed. Add trimming, if desired. Stitch small pocket over large pocket where indicated on pattern.

3) Appliqué (see page 10) babushka fronts and backs to matching doll fronts and backs. Appliqué faces over babushka fronts, tucking in a small bit of stuffing before taking last stitches. Embroider hair and facial features (see page 10). Add trimming to bodies, if desired.

4) Stitch large pocket to large doll front where indicated on pattern. With right sides facing, stitch doll front to back, leaving lower edges open. Stitch circular base to lower edge, leaving 4" open. Clip curves, turn right side out, and stuff. Stitch opening closed.

5) With right sides facing, stitch smaller doll fronts to backs, leaving lower edges open. Turn right side out, stuff, and stitch openings closed. Slip dolls into pockets.

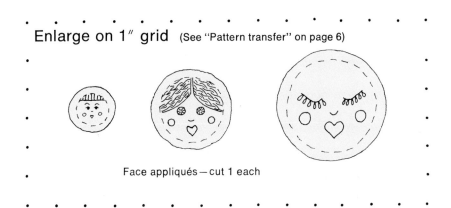

Enlarge on 1" grid (See "Pattern transfer" on page 6)

Face appliqués—cut 1 each

BYZANTIUM in patchwork, our Matryoshka Mama carries her children in pockets.

Matryoshka: Enlarge on 1″ grid ● ¼″ seam allowance

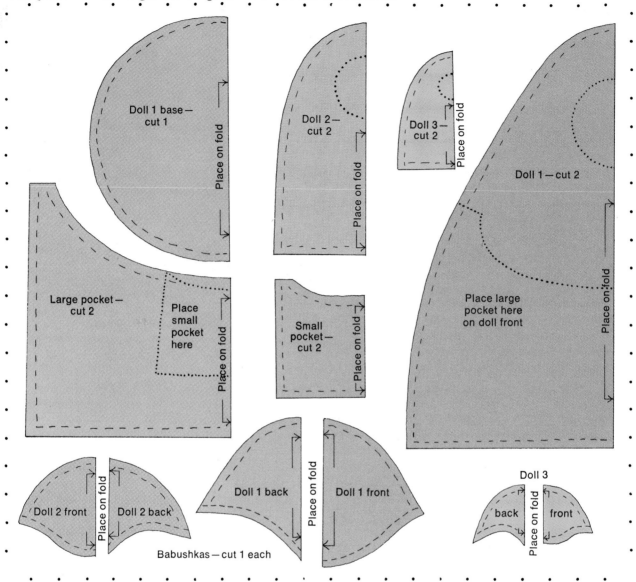

Doll 1 base — cut 1
Place on fold

Doll 2 — cut 2
Place on fold

Doll 3 — cut 2
Place on fold

Doll 1 — cut 2

Large pocket — cut 2

Place small pocket here
Place on fold

Small pocket — cut 2
Place on fold

Place large pocket here on doll front
Place on fold

Doll 2 front   Doll 2 back
Place on fold

Doll 1 back   Doll 1 front
Place on fold

Babushkas — cut 1 each

Doll 3
back   front
Place on fold

(See "Pattern transfer" on page 6)

IN 19TH CENTURY RUSSIA, holding the mama doll meant you might be blessed with children or grandchildren. Directions start on page 35.

Papoose babies

ONE BABY gets a fatherly tickle.

Here is a cute, simple little dolly that arrives papoose-style in its own sleeping bag. Any small mother would fall in love with it on sight. It is hardly more than a round bundle — just the size children like to wrap up in a diaper or small blanket of their own making. And this project is so simple to make, you might even opt for two — as we did.

You'll need: For *each* 14-inch doll, ½ yard lightweight cotton; ½ yard *each* quilted fabric and cotton flannel for sleeping bag and lining; ½ yard eyelet ruffle; thread to match fabrics; scraps of yarn and felt for hair and mouth; 2 buttons for eyes; 1 bag polyester stuffing.

Putting it together

1) Enlarge and transfer patterns (right) for doll and sleeping bag. Cut doll front and back from lightweight cotton; cut sleeping bag and lining from quilted fabric and cotton flannel.

2) With right sides facing, stitch doll front to doll back, making ¼" seam and leaving open between notches. Clip at neck, turn right side out, stuff, and stitch closed. Sew on button eyes; glue or sew on felt crescent mouth. Add yarn hair (to make loop curls, see page 15).

3) With right sides together, stitch sleeping bag to its lining along both long sides and curved end, making ¼" seam and leaving open between A and B. Clip curves; turn right side out.

4) Matching straight edges at open end of bag, stitch eyelet ruffle close to edge of lining fabric through both thicknesses. Trim seam and fold 2" over quilted fabric (like folded top sheet of a bed). Stitch ruffle close to edge of lining to hold fold in place.

5) With lining on outside, fold bag along line indicated on pattern. Stitch along sides, making ¼" seams. Turn right side out. Slip doll inside.

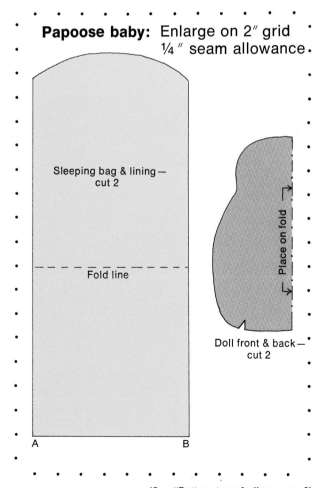

Papoose baby: Enlarge on 2" grid ¼" seam allowance

Sleeping bag & lining — cut 2

Fold line

A   B

Place on fold

Doll front & back — cut 2

(See "Pattern transfer" on page 6)

Topsy-turvy storyteller

With a flip of her skirts and a flick of your wrist, this doll suddenly switches roles. She has two heads—one at each end of her body. Each head has two faces, making a total of four storytelling roles. This favorite folk toy of generations of children was re-created for us by Jean Heighton.

Our topsy-turvy doll's multiple personality includes sweet Red Riding Hood, scared Red Riding Hood, Grandma, and the Wicked Wolf. You could substitute a number of other folk tale characters (many stories, like *Cinderella,* need only two roles).

You'll need: For body and hands—½ yard sturdy cotton or cotton blend fabric; for clothing (use lightweight fabric)—1 yard white, ½ yard red, ¾ yard print; 3 yards lace; ½ yard ribbon; ½ yard of ¼-inch elastic cord; 1 gray felt square plus red and white felt scraps for Wolf's face; 9 buttons for eyes and for Wolf's nose; embroidery floss for features; red, white, and gray thread; gray and yellow yarn for hair; 1 bag polyester stuffing.

Putting it together

1) Enlarge and transfer patterns (page 40) and cut out—body and hands from sturdy cotton; dress pieces (arms, sleeve caps, bodices) from *both* white and print fabric plus an 18 by 32″ rectangle from *each* for skirts; two 12″ circles for caps from red and two from white fabric; two 8 by 10″ rectangles from red fabric for cape; Wolf's face from gray felt.

2) Join body pieces, right sides together, leaving 3″ opening in top of each head (all seams are ¼″). Turn right side out; stuff. (Note: Because doll will lead a life of somersaults, stuff *firmly,* especially at necks and waist.) Stitch head openings closed.

3) Fold print and white arms lengthwise, right sides together. Stitch along wrist ends and underarms, leaving tops open. Stitch hand fronts to backs, leaving wrists open. Turn arms and hands right side out, and stuff. Fit hands over sewn ends of arms, tuck under raw edges, and stitch in place. Trim with lace. Tuck in raw edges of upper arms; stitch securely to body.

4) Stitch darts in bodice fronts and backs. Sew shoulder seams, right sides together. Cut 1 side of each bodice down center from neck to waist. Gather 1 long edge of each sleeve cap. Adjust gathers to fit, pin sleeve caps to bodice armholes, right sides together, and stitch. Stitch side seams of bodices and underarm seams of sleeve caps. Turn right side out. Dress doll, matching bodices to arms. Hem and gather sleeve cap openings to fit snugly around arms. Slipstitch in place. Stitch bodice openings closed. Cover stitching and trim necklines with lace.

5) Fold skirt rectangles in half, right sides together, widthwise; stitch back seams. Hem raw edges; trim bottom edge with lace. Gather each waist, pulling tight after slipping skirt on matching end of doll. Stitch skirt waistlines to bodices.

6) Baste Wolf's face between A and B (see sketch, page 40). Baste triangular jaw gusset between nose and sides of face (B to C). Stitch over basting; turn right side out and stuff. Place over 1 face at Grandma's end of doll. Stitch to head, adding stuffing as you work.

7) Make hair by wrapping yarn around ruler (see page 15), creating "fringe" with looped ends (1 ruler length of yellow yarn and 2 lengths of gray). Stitch down 1 side of ruler to hold strands together. Slip ruler out. Attach to heads along center head seams.

8) Make caps by stitching matching circles right sides together, leaving 1″ openings. Turn right side out and stitch closed. Make casing for elastic by stitching in a circle 1″ from perimeter of each cap. Stitch again ¼″ inside 1st stitching. Snip through 1 thickness of fabric and insert elastic cord (attach safety pin to maneuver through fabric). Pull elastic, gathering caps to fit heads; stitch ends together. Sew caps securely at sides of each to matching head.

9) Hem edges of 2 cape pieces. Gather 1 long edge of each. Adjust gathers to fit neatly around

DELIGHT a small child with a doll that flip-flops to tell a favorite story.

Red Riding Hood's shoulders. Stitch in place; add ribbon bows.

10) Embroider faces, using split stitch for lines, satin stitch for filling (see page 10). Give Red Riding Hood a frightened expression on 1 face (raised eyebrows, perhaps an O-shaped mouth). Sew button eyes to faces and button nose to Wolf. Stitch felt teeth and tongue to Wolf's face; make French knots around his nose.

Topsy-turvy doll: Enlarge on 1″ grid • ¼″ seam allowance (See "Pattern transfer" on page 6)

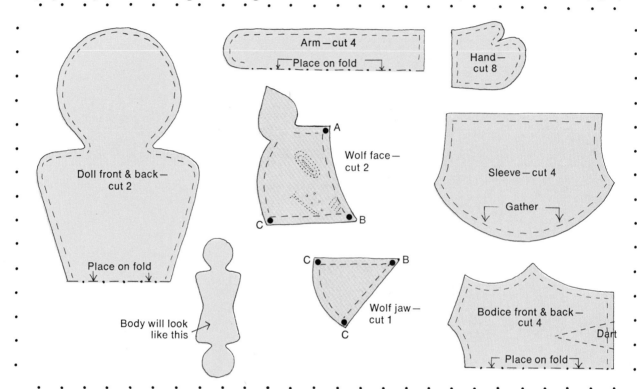

Wolf's face

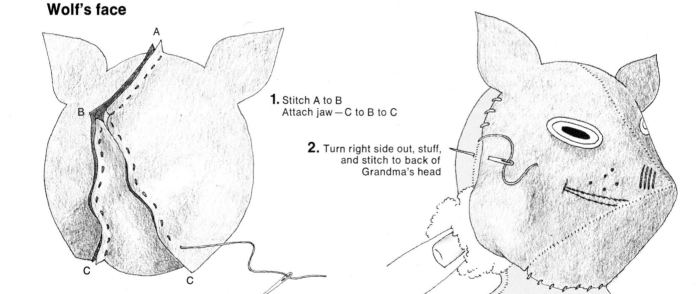

1. Stitch A to B
Attach jaw — C to B to C

2. Turn right side out, stuff, and stitch to back of Grandma's head

Batik beauties

(Photo on page 42)

If you're a novice to batik, you might like to try this ancient dyeing craft on a small scale first. Applying batik to doll designs can reward you with happy surprises — Maud and Nelly on the next page are two colorful examples of what can happen. They were designed by Barbara di Conza.

See page 11 for a detailed explanation of how to batik. Basically what you do is paint or print a design on cotton fabric with melted wax. After the wax hardens, you immerse the fabric in a dyebath which tints the areas left uncoated.

You'll need: For *each* doll approximately the size of ours (Maud is 24 inches tall, Nelly is 16 inches) — ½ yard muslin (be *sure* to preshrink so fabric will absorb dyes properly); ½ yard printed cotton for backing; 2 or 3 permanent cold-water dyes in harmonious colors or different shades of 1 color (we used aqua/purple and salmon/purple); 8 ounces of premixed batik wax or 4 ounces *each* of paraffin wax and beeswax; inexpensive natural-bristle brushes for applying wax or odds and ends such as thread spools for printing wax designs; batik thickener (from art supplier) and red dye for painted cheeks (optional); double boiler or cans to hold chunks of wax and cooking pot large enough to hold cans; plastic or enamel dishpan for dyebath; artist's stretcher bars or large picture frame to stretch fabric; 1 bag polyester stuffing.

Putting it together

1) Draw your own pattern or enlarge and transfer ours (page 43). A simple way to draw your own is to fold a large sheet of paper in half. Using fold as doll's center line, draw only half the figure. Cut through both layers and unfold.

2) Using carbon paper, trace this symmetrical body shape (or our pattern) onto muslin. Pin same pattern to wrong side of backing fabric, and cut out doll back.

3) If you want to follow guidelines rather than apply wax freehand, pencil these lightly on muslin. Stretch muslin tight between stretcher bars or around picture frame.

4) Following instructions on page 11, coat areas you want to remain white with melted wax, brushing it on or printing it with spools and other small objects. Read instructions on dye packets. Immerse muslin in palest dye. After it has dried, apply more wax to those portions of dyed area you want to remain the pale shade. Immerse muslin in darker dye (which will combine with pale shade where it is uncoated with wax).

5) If you wish, you can paint details such as pink cheeks after final dye has dried. Mix a little red dye with thickener according to package directions (thickener prevents dye from "bleeding" into fabric). Test color on fabric scrap before painting doll.

6) To remove wax, cover fabric with paper towels and press with warm iron. Soak in boiling soapy water to melt away last traces of wax. Rinse thoroughly and dry.

7) Press fabric smooth and cut out doll, adding ½" seam allowance all around. With right sides together, stitch batik doll to backing, leaving 3" opening in 1 side. Clip curves and corners. Turn right side out, stuff, and stitch opening closed.

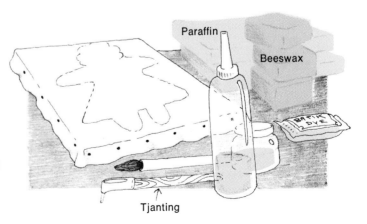

Paraffin

Beeswax

Tjanting

Batik beauties: Enlarge on 1″ grid
¼″ seam allowance

(See ''Pattern transfer'' on page 6)

Trace on muslin for batik front

Cut doll backs, laying pattern on wrong side of coordinating fabric

*PLUMP NELLY and svelte Maud
saunter out to walk the dog.
Directions start on page 41.*

*PAPA DOLL or whimsical sculpture? Created entirely from pantyhose, he soaks in a quilted tub with seashell feet. Tiny puppet faces (**below**) are sewn to finger tips of an elegant glove.*

Stitch sculptures from nylon stockings

These soft "people" come to life as you stitch through their padding, bulging their nylon skin here, sucking in a dimple there. Often they are incredibly unbeautiful — maybe this is the secret of their charm. So realistic are they that at first glance they may look hard to make. But not so. The only real snag is that nylons do — all too often. For children's toys you could substitute scraps from thick tights or a T-shirt.

Our gallery of dolls includes the work of Phyllis Dunstan ("Grandma"), Jean Ferris (glove puppets and trio of beanbags), and Joan Schulze ("Father" in the tub, "the Boys," and "Angel").

GRANDMA AND THE BOYS (left) line up for a few bars of sweet harmony. Beanbags in triplicate (middle) have appliqué faces. Lady's pink body is purchased fuzzy slipper; Indian's is car chamois. Satin stitches embossing eyes and lips add delicate color to angel's ethereal beauty (lower).

You'll need: Pantyhose or stockings in good condition (stretchy mesh is easiest to work with) and matching thread; long needle (#1 sharp or #1 crewel); embroidery floss or beads for detail; fluffy material for hair (see page 15 for ideas); fabric scraps and thrift store trimmings for clothing; polyester fiber or cotton wool.

Putting it together

1) From nylon, cut an oblong tube about twice as big as you want head to be. Slit tube open and fill with stuffing. Fold long sides over stuffing and tie short sides in style of hobo's bundle: this is back of head.

2) Start with nose. Knot thread at back of head. Pass needle to front, coming up at top of nose area and to one side. With next stitch, push needle under a tuft of stuffing to opposite side of nose area. As you pull tight, nose begins to bulge. Continue back and forth down length of nose, creating a fleshy ridge. Leave nostril area open or define it with a horizontal row of stitches.

3) Stitch narrower ridges to form eyelids, lips, or furrows of age. To make dimples, stitch through head, pull tight, and knot thread at back.

4) Brighten eyes with French knots or satin stitches (see page 10), or with beads. Add satin-stitched luster to lips, if you like.

5) A simple body can be quite effective. Sew an oval or arch-shaped beanbag of fabric scraps. Stitch around rim of face to fasten to front of beanbag. Attach tiny heads to finger tips of glove to make a family of puppets. To go further afield, consider Father in his bath (opposite page) — he is made entirely of pantyhose tubes, stuffed and modeled with stitches. His tub is a rectangle of quilted fabric, seamed up the back, gathered at the base, and glued to cardboard.

Dolls: Stitch sculptures **45**

An animal kingdom

Most children become attached, at some time, to a fluffy, cuddly toy animal. The species may range from one end of the animal kingdom to the other — but whether the favorite creature is a teddy bear or an octopus, the affection bestowed is the same. On the next 20 pages you'll find a bevy of beasts to make for your children or yourself. Some are as small as lap dogs, others big enough to ride. Most of them are furry. All are soft and huggable.

William walrus

This toothy charmer would melt and conquer anyone's heart. Lovingly made of purple felt and fondly bedecked with a yarn mustache, our walrus is ready to flap his flippers and slither into your lap. He was designed by Francoise Kirkman.

Make your walrus from felt in your favorite warm-blooded color. Choose a shade of yarn that contrasts boisterously. Then, when he's finished, find him a warm-blooded, boisterous playmate.

You'll need: For a 20-inch-long walrus — ½ yard felt; scraps of contrasting felt for eyes and nose; 2 white felt squares for tusks; thread to match felt (or dental floss); bright yarn scraps for mustache; 1 bag polyester stuffing.

Putting him together

1) Enlarge and transfer pattern (facing page) for walrus. Cut body and flipper pieces from doubled felt. Cut tusks from white felt.

2) As indicated on pattern, stitch curved dart (his "chin") in underbody gusset.

3) Baste and stitch side pieces together between forehead and tail, A to B (all seams are ¼"). Pair and stitch flipper pieces, leaving open between C and D. Turn right side out. Baste each flipper to right side of walrus side where indicated on pattern. Baste and stitch gusset to sides, matching A and B, leaving opening between notches on one side.

4) Pair and stitch together tusk pieces, leaving straight sides open. Turn body and tusks so that seams are on inside. Stitch across body where indicated on pattern to separate tail.

5) Stuff body and tusks. Using strong thread or dental floss, blindstitch tusks in place. Glue on felt eyes, nose.

6) For mustache, thickly wrap yarn around ruler for length of 4½" (see sketch, page 15). Stitch to catch each strand of yarn along length of ruler. Slip ruler out; trim yarn loops to desired mustache length. Blindstitch to walrus, sewing over previous stitching.

WARM, WOOLY WALRUS is an ice melter from the Far North.

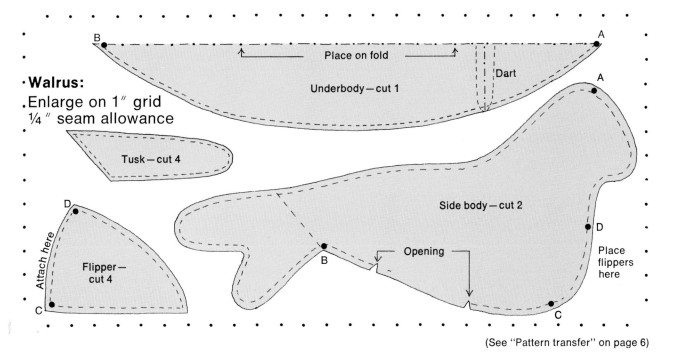

B   Place on fold   A

Dart

Walrus:
Enlarge on 1″ grid
¼″ seam allowance

Underbody—cut 1

A

Tusk—cut 4

Side body—cut 2

D

Attach here

D

Opening

Place flippers here

Flipper— cut 4

B

C

C

(See ''Pattern transfer'' on page 6)

Animals: Walrus   47

A rabbit duo

Here are two unusual bunnies for Easter — or any other occasion when a rabbit might come in handy. Each was put together from fabric scraps and thrift store "finds."

The long-legged, floppy creature (shown opposite lounging on a bed of carrots) is an old T-shirt, reincarnated by Lynne Morrall. His bunny puppet cousin was fashioned by Jean Ferris from a castoff suede glove. Either one is sure to delight rabbit lovers of any age.

You'll need: For the 29-inch floppy rabbit — 1 man's T-shirt; deep pink and blue embroidery floss; 1 pair child's knee socks; white pompon from curtain fringe; polyester stuffing; white thread. For puppet — 1 soft glove; scrap of T-shirt or other knit fabric for face; embroidery floss; dark thread and tiny beads for features; small amount polyester stuffing.

Floppy rabbit

1) Enlarge and transfer pattern (facing page), and cut out from T-shirt. With right sides together, stitch front to back, making ¼″ seam, leaving 3″ opening in head. Turn right side out; stuff, using dowel or chopstick to reach extremities. Stitch head opening closed. Sew on pompon tail.

2) Stitch to quilt ears and feet as indicated on pattern. To create contours of face, handstitch from 1 side of upper nose to other, using white thread; pass needle under stuffing, drawing stitches tight. Continue down length of nose. Use same technique to make cheeks bulge. With embroidery floss, go over outline of lower halves of cheeks, ending in peak under tip of nose. Make blue nose and pink eyes with satin stitches (see page 10 on embroidery).

3) To make cap, use toe of 1 sock cut off 3″ from tip. Tuck under raw edge and stitch to rabbit's head. Push down center of cap; stitch to head with embroidery floss, making tassel with thread ends.

4) To make sweater, cut off upper sections of both socks — one 7½″ long and one 3½″ long (including ribbing). Hem raw edge of longer section and cut 1″ armholes ¾″ below ribbing. (Embroider name on front, if you wish.) Slip over rabbit, pulling arms through openings, folding sock cuff for turtleneck. Cut smaller section into 2 rectangles to make sleeves with ribbing at wrists. Fit snugly around rabbit's arms. Stitch underarm and armhole seams by hand.

Bunny puppet

1) Make face by cutting circle 4″ in diameter from scrap of T-shirt or other knit fabric. Baste around perimeter to gather. Put small handful of stuffing into center of wrong side. Draw gathers tight to close edge of circle around stuffing; knot thread securely.

2) Embroider features (see page 10). Our bunny's eyes are tiny black beads; lashes and whiskers are sketched with long stitches of brown thread; nose and mouth are chain stitched with brown floss; cheeks are flushed with light dabs of lipstick.

3) Lay face over upper palm of glove. With pencil, lightly trace around it, keeping just inside edge of face. Cut traced circle out of glove. Fit face inside opening, turn raw edge under, and stitch in place.

4) Push index and little fingers of glove to inside. Stuff 2 middle fingers and thumb. Latter becomes rabbit's right arm — fold it toward chest and stitch in place so he can hold bouquet.

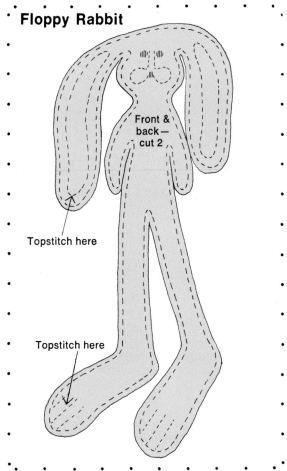

Floppy Rabbit

Front &
back —
cut 2

Topstitch here

Topstitch here

Enlarge on 2″ grid ● ¼″ seam allowance

(See "Pattern transfer" on page 6)

*FLOPPY PETER (above) sports a monogrammed
turtleneck sewn from a knee sock. Bunny with bouquet
(right) puts new life into an old suede glove.*

Knee sock zoo

You start with the incredible, stretchable sock. Colorful, cuddly, cheap, and—best of all—tubular, socks are a marvelous resource for toy makers. All you do is cut them, stuff them, and mix up the pieces until they no longer look like feet.

What *do* they look like? We offer a few reassembled sock creations that look like a rooster, a fish, an elephant, and a hobbylion (who, with a shift of the mane, becomes a hobbyhorse). Most of these toys are made from knee socks, chosen for their generous proportions, bright colors, and the option of separated toes.

Our zoo is the work of Suki Graef (hobbylion) and Francoise Kirkman (rooster, fish, and elephant).

You'll need: Prewashed socks — for rooster and fish, 1 pair of 23-inch knee socks with separated toes for *each* animal; for elephant, one 17-inch knee sock (if your socks are different lengths, don't worry—just make sure animals' legs match); for hobbylion, 1 very large man's work sock; felt squares for trim; 4-ounce skein of yarn for lion's mane; embroidery floss to match felt and sock colors; 1 bag polyester stuffing for *each* animal; for hobbylion, broomstick with rubber crutch tip.

Putting them together

1) Following sketches below, cut pair of socks for rooster. Cut pair of socks for fish, single sock for elephant or hobbylion, following sketches on pages 52 and 53.

2) Rooster: Stuff cockscomb (toes of 1 sock) and body. Tuck in raw edges of legs and stitch inner leg seam. Stuff legs. To close, gather openings, pull tight, and knot thread. Bind ankles with yarn or embroidery floss. Stuff tail (toes and foot of other sock). Tuck in raw edge and stitch to body. Bind 4″ from tail feather. Stitch triangular felt pieces (beak) down 2 long sides. Stuff and sew to face. Stitch or glue on felt eyes (we used 3 concentric circles of contrasting colors).

3) Fish: Stuff tail and body. To close mouth end, gather, pull tight, and knot thread. Bind tail 5″ from big toe. Stuff top fin, tuck in raw edge, and stitch to body. Stitch 4 triangular felt pieces (side fins) in 2 pairs down long sides. Stuff and sew to lower sides of body. Stitch together 2 circular felt mouth pieces around edge, leaving small opening. Stuff and finish stitching. Using contrasting embroidery floss, sew through center to fish. Stitch or glue on felt eyes.

(Continued on page 52)

Rooster

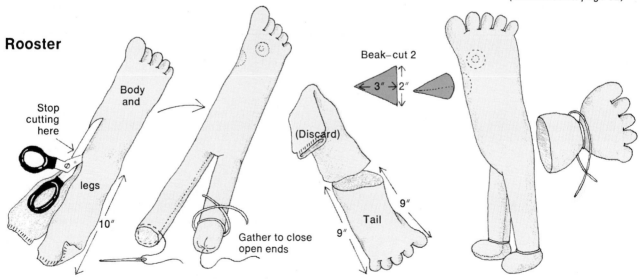

ROOSTER, elephant, and fish (left)
and hungry lion (below) are just
a few of the creatures you
can sew from socks.

4) Elephant: Stuff body (foot and lower ankle of sock). Tuck in raw edges of hind legs, stitch inner leg seam, and stuff. To close, gather openings, pull tight, and knot thread. Fold each front leg piece in half lengthwise. Stitch down side and 1 end. Stuff and sew legs to body. After cutting angle in trunk piece as shown in sketch, stitch down length. Stuff and sew to chin area. Stitch 4 triangular felt tusks in 2 pairs down long sides. Stuff and sew to face at sides of trunk.

For ears, cut 2 half-circles of felt in contrasting colors. Cut both in half. Stitch contrasting pieces together down curved side and 1 straight side. Stuff and sew to head. Fold felt tail piece in half lengthwise. Fringe 1 end. Stitch across tail just above fringe and down length. Attach to body. Sew or glue on felt eyes.

5) Hobbylion: Start with his roaring mouth. Fold mouth piece in half, matching curved edges. Slide tongue inside with straight edge against fold. Stitch across top, parallel to fold and close to it, to hold tongue in place. Open mouth; with tongue side facing, baste teeth around curved edges with points turned inward. After cutting 4″ slit in toe of sock, turn this portion inside out. Join slit edge to mouth, stretching sock to fit, right sides together. Turn right side out again.

Pin loops of yarn for mane around cut edge at sock heel. Turn ankle portion of sock inside out and pull over toe portion, matching raw edges. Stitch ½″ seam, securing mane and joining toe and ankle halves. Turn ankle right side out again. Stuff; insert broomstick into neck and finish stuffing. Tie off at base of neck; staple sock to broomstick. Sew felt nose tip to nose, right sides together, along straight edge (A to B). Turn and appliqué to lion, stuffing as you stitch. Lay felt inner ear pieces over ears. Fold each ear so that inner ear is inside. Stitch parallel to fold, making ear cup; attach to lion.

Glue or sew on felt eyes; add yarn tassel to chin.

Variation: Use colorful socks to make stitch-sculptured dolls, following directions for nylon stocking dolls on page 45.

Elephant

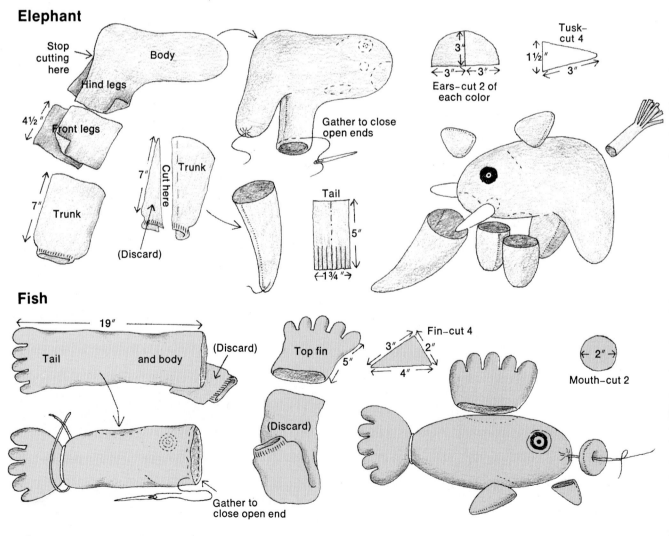

Stop cutting here

Body

Hind legs

4½″

Front legs

7″ Trunk

7″ Cut here Trunk

(Discard)

Gather to close open ends

Tail

5″

←1¾″→

3″

3″ ← 3″ →

Ears–cut 2 of each color

Tusk– cut 4

1½″

3″

Fish

←— 19″ —→

Tail and body

(Discard)

Gather to close open end

Top fin

5″

(Discard)

Fin–cut 4

3″ 2″

4″

← 2″ →

Mouth–cut 2

Hobby lion

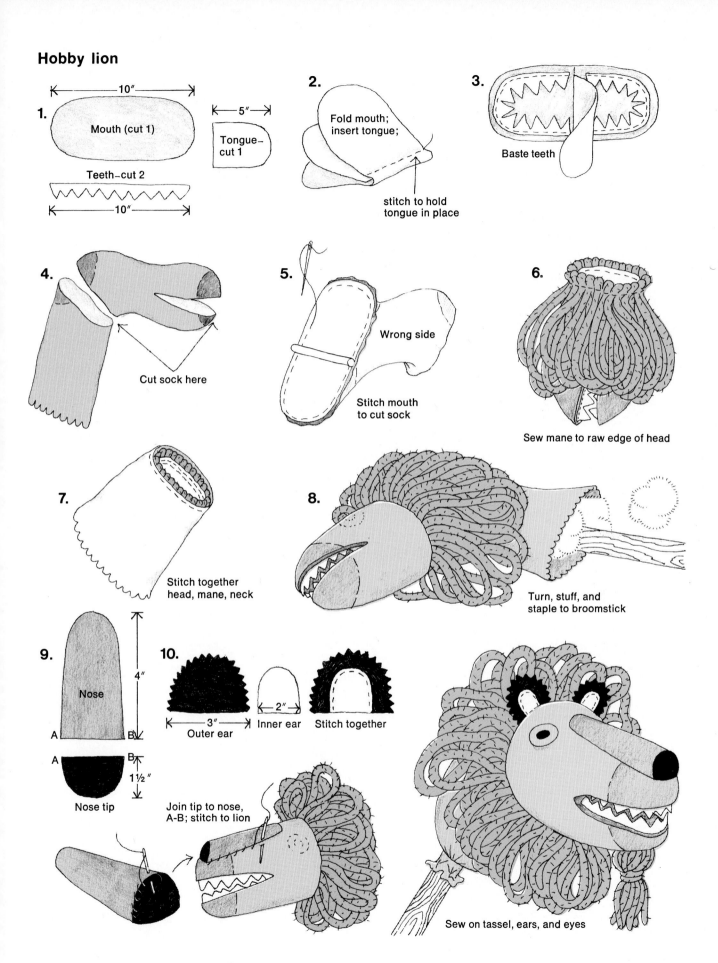

1. 10"

Mouth (cut 1)

5"

Tongue – cut 1

Teeth – cut 2

10"

2. Fold mouth; insert tongue; stitch to hold tongue in place

3. Baste teeth

4. Cut sock here

5. Wrong side

Stitch mouth to cut sock

6. Sew mane to raw edge of head

7. Stitch together head, mane, neck

8. Turn, stuff, and staple to broomstick

9. Nose

4"

A B

Nose tip

A B

1½"

10. Outer ear 3"   Inner ear 2"   Stitch together

Join tip to nose, A-B; stitch to lion

Sew on tassel, ears, and eyes

Animals: Knee sock zoo **53**

THREE FURRY PETS get together for communal dining.

Bean bag fluff to cuddle or toss

Here are three creatures, each from a different neck of the woods — the beaver, the rabbit, and the cat. What they have in common are coats of soft, strokable fur and simple, crouching body shapes. You can make all three (plus any other furry, low-bellied animal you fancy) from one basic design by Francoise Kirkman.

You'll need: For *each* 12-inch animal (excluding tails) — ¼ yard fake fur; felt scraps in contrasting colors for features; 3 gray felt squares for beaver; three 5-inch strips of black felt or plastic for cat's whiskers; 3 white pompons for rabbit's eyes and nose; scraps of white fake fur or fluffy velour to trim rabbit and cat; birdseed and styrofoam pellets or 2 bags polyester stuffing (for 3 animals).

Putting them together

1) Enlarge and transfer patterns (facing page) for body and top head/underbody (same for each animal). Make templates (see page 12). Cut pieces from fake fur. Enlarge and transfer ear, paw, and tail patterns for animal of your choice:
- **Beaver's** ears are cut twice from gray felt, twice from fake fur; feet and tail are felt.
- **Rabbit's** ears and paws are cut twice from body fur, twice from white fur (or velour); tail is cut once from body fur, once from white fur or velour.
- **Cat's** ears are cut twice from body fur, twice from white fur or velour; feet are cut from white fur or velour; tail is cut from body fur.

2) Right sides together, pin underbody to sides, matching letters A, B, and C and notches. Baste, then stitch (all seams are ¼"), leaving 1 side open between notches. Stitch sides together, A to C. Clip seam at curves and corners.

3) Turn body right side out and stuff. We poured styrofoam pellets through a funnel to fill most of each animal, with final layer of birdseed to fill belly (when tossed, animals land on their feet because birdseed is heavier than styrofoam). Or you can use polyester stuffing alone. When filled, stitch opening closed (if birdseed was used, take tiny stitches to prevent leaks).

4) Rabbit: Pair tail, ear, and paw pieces (be sure that 1 of *each* pair is white), right sides together. Stitch, leaving straight sides open; turn right side out, and stuff tail *only.* With raw edges tucked inside and white side down, sew short paws to front of underbody, long paws (slanting to each side) to rear of underbody. Gather ear openings, after tucking in raw edges. Sew ears close together at back of head, with white sides facing out. Attach tail, with white side facing down. Sew on white pompon nose and eyes. Glue on felt pupils.

5) Cat: Pair tail, ear, and leg pieces, making sure 1 side of *each* ear is white. With right sides together, stitch each pair, leaving straight sides open. Turn right side out; stuff legs *only.* Stitch short legs to front of underbody, long ones to rear. Attach tail and ears, with whites of ears facing front. Add felt facial features. Position whiskers under nose and stitch in place.

6) Beaver: Pair ears, right sides together, and stitch, leaving straight sides open. Turn right side out and sew to sides of head. Lay felt tail and feet pieces together. Topstitch close to edge. Topstitch diamonds on tail and ribs on feet as indicated on pattern. Stitch short feet to front underbody, long feet to rear. Attach tail, felt eyes, nose, and 2 rectangular teeth.

Bean Bag Fluff: Enlarge on 1″ grid • ¼″ seam allowance (See "Pattern transfer" on page 6)

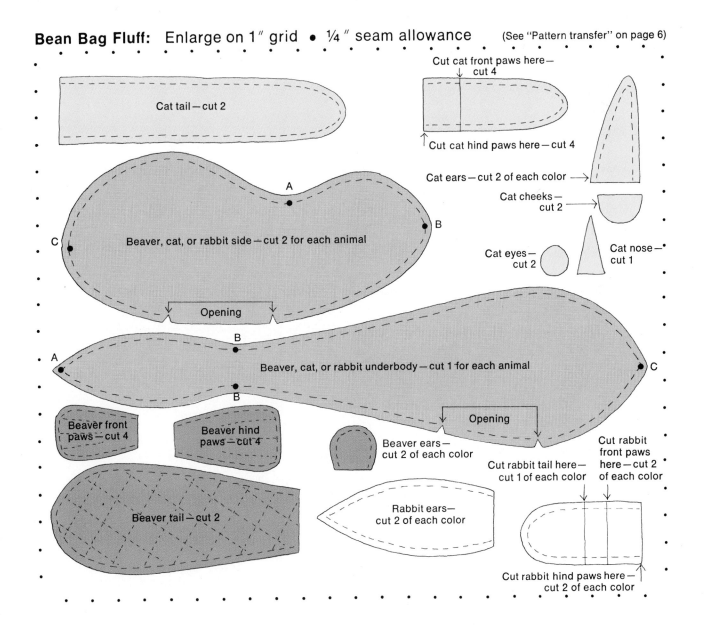

Cat tail—cut 2

Cut cat front paws here— cut 4

Cut cat hind paws here—cut 4

Cat ears—cut 2 of each color →

Cat cheeks— cut 2

Cat eyes— cut 2

Cat nose— cut 1

Beaver, cat, or rabbit side—cut 2 for each animal

Opening

Beaver, cat, or rabbit underbody—cut 1 for each animal

Opening

Beaver front paws—cut 4

Beaver hind paws—cut 4

Beaver ears— cut 2 of each color

Cut rabbit front paws here—cut 2 of each color

Cut rabbit tail here— cut 1 of each color

Beaver tail—cut 2

Rabbit ears— cut 2 of each color

Cut rabbit hind paws here— cut 2 of each color

"BUTTERFLIES are pretty and some can fly fast. This one's name is Floppy."—Sean Flanagan.

"I LIKE my big cat. She's pretty-white so I call her Marshmallow."—Mary Wadsworth (above). "He's really a special worm. He has a flower sticking out of his fuzzy hat."—Elana Lombard (right).

Animals: Child art pillows

"MY CHICK is nice and round and fuzzy. I call her Vanilla Furry Smith."—Katie Smith.

"MY LION'S name is Daisy Lullaby because he's yellow and he likes to sleep."—Anna Lee.

Child art pillow toys

Children do the paperwork for this project. Your job is to enlarge their drawings, cut them out of fabric, and stitch them up.

The gallery of soft sculptures shown here represents the fantasies of children come to life. Details on appliqué and stitchery techniques can be found in Chapter 1. Note that the butterfly (opposite page) has no added detail—bright fabric alone conveys its spirit.

You'll need: Simple child's drawing for *each* toy; enough fabric to cut identical front and back, using enlarged drawing as pattern; thread to match as well as to contrast for stitchery, if used; contrasting fabric or felt scraps for appliqué, if used; 2 bags polyester stuffing for large toy (or 1 bag foam chips for pillow).

Putting them together

1) Start with simple child's drawing. If it is very big, use drawing itself as pattern. Otherwise, rule a grid of small squares over drawing and copy on graph paper with larger grid (see page 6 for details on transferring).

2) Pin to doubled fabric (right sides together) and cut front and back from both thicknesses. Lightly transfer to right side of front piece any marks to show placement of appliqués, if used. Also transfer guidelines for embroidery (unless you prefer freehand stitchery).

3) Appliqué and stitch details on front of animal. Zigzag stitch to indicate thick lines. Or simply glue on details (such as white vinyl polka dots on green vinyl worm, opposite page).

4) When front is finished, pin to back, right sides together. Stitch ¼ to ½″ seam (depending on size of toy) all around, leaving 6″ opening in 1 side. Turn right side out. Stuff with foam chips for squishy pillow (see page 6 for coping with mess) or with polyester stuffing for soft toy. Stitch opening closed.

Bouncy foam-filled beasts

It is nearly impossible to sit still on these lovable foam-filled creatures. They jiggle and bounce, buck and spring, fueled by the jumping beans of their 4 to 10-year-old riders.

Created by Francoise Kirkman, each chunky animal is carved from a solid block of foam and then upholstered in fuzzy fabric. Making one is not difficult—though stuffing the large foam shape into its "hide" requires a bit of dexterity and perseverance.

Check the Yellow Pages under "Rubber— Foam and Sponge" for suppliers of polyurethane foam. Each of our animals began as a block 30 inches long, 17 inches high, and 10 inches deep, cut by the supplier with the strongest pressure resistance in the height so that the animal would stay firm under a child's weight.

You'll need: For *each* animal—block of foam (see details above) and 1½ yards of 60-inch-wide velour or fake fur; scraps of contrasting fabric and felt for horns, ears, and eyes; thread to match fabric; two 4-ounce skeins of yarn for pony's mane and tail; 1 package iron-on patches to reinforce stress points; white glue or special glue for foam (available where foam is sold, it creates a more flexible bond but is rather expensive); heavy-duty thread; curved upholstery needle; polyester stuffing for ears, horns, and tail; electric carving knife, bread knife, or band saw for cutting foam.

Putting them together

1) Enlarge and transfer 1 of the patterns (page 61) to wrapping paper. Separate rectangular feet patterns. As shown in sketches, page 60, lay body and head pattern on broad side of foam block; trace with felt-tip pen. Repeat on opposite side. Draw across width of block at nose and top of head.

2) Using electric carving knife or similar tool, cut through foam, following penned outline. Slice section taken from under animal's chin to make 2 blocks for front and hind feet. Glue these to foam body; allow to dry overnight.

3) Reinforce stress places where ears, horns, and tail will be attached by ironing adhesive patches to foam (shield foam from heat with sheets of paper).

4) Tape feet patterns to body and head pattern. Fold fabric in half, right sides together, with selvages meeting. Pin pattern to both thicknesses, leaving room across width of fabric for 2 strips, each 11 by 60". Cut out pattern, adding ½" all around for seam allowance. Cut out strips; cut out ear and horn (4 *each*), and tail pieces (2 *each*) from body fabric or contrasting scraps.

5) Stitch eyes in place, using stuffed appliqué (see page 10), felt, or buttons. Our hippo's nostrils and smile are indicated with zigzag machine stitching.

6) Join long strips, right sides together, along 11" ends. Matching point A on body sides with seam in strip, pin and baste strip to sides, right sides together. Work toward front and back underbody, leaving belly open between C and D (pony requires a large opening, to bottom of feet, because its legs are longer). As you baste, check that side pieces are identically placed along center strip. Stitch curved dart across center strip at point B (to prevent a sagging chin), tapering from nothing to ½" at center, and back to nothing. Machine stitch over basting.

7) Cut excess fabric off strip between C and D, leaving just enough to close opening. Clip corners and dart. Turn cover right side out. Stuff foam shape, head and front paws first, into cover (squeeze foam hard to compact; it helps to sit on it). Handstitch underbody closed.

(Continued on page 60)

CLIMB ABOARD for a wild ride. Carved foam beasts are not only bouncy, but lightweight as well (pillow fight anyone?).

Animals: Bouncy beasts **59**

8) Pair ear, horn, and tail pieces right sides together. Stitch, stuff with polyester stuffing, and sew to animal, passing needle through adhesive patches for extra strength.

9) To make pony's mane, wrap yarn thickly around a 10″-long book; sew down middle of each side of book; cut yarn along edges. Make thick braid of yarn; sew mane to braid, and sew braid to pony's head and neck. Wrap yarn around a longer book to make tail; tie one end and cut the other; stitch to hindquarters, passing needle through adhesive patch.

Working with foam

1. Trace pattern on foam with felt tip pen

2. Carve with bread knife, band saw, or electric carving knife

3. Glue blocks cut from under chin for animal's feet

4. Iron-on adhesive patches, masking foam with sheet of paper

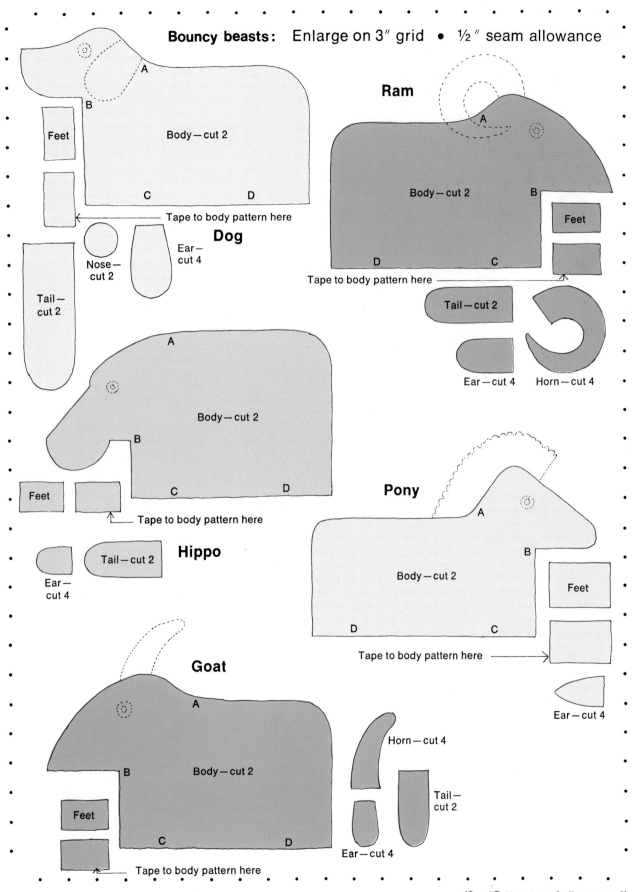

Bouncy beasts: Enlarge on 3″ grid ● ½″ seam allowance

Dog

Body—cut 2

A

B

Feet

C   D

Tape to body pattern here

Nose—cut 2

Tail—cut 2

Ear—cut 4

Ram

A

Body—cut 2

B

D   C

Feet

Tape to body pattern here

Tail—cut 2

Ear—cut 4   Horn—cut 4

Hippo

A

Body—cut 2

B

C   D

Feet

Tape to body pattern here

Ear—cut 4

Tail—cut 2

Pony

A

Body—cut 2

B

D   C

Feet

Tape to body pattern here

Ear—cut 4

Goat

A

Body—cut 2

B

Feet

C   D

Tape to body pattern here

Horn—cut 4

Tail—cut 2

Ear—cut 4

(See ''Pattern transfer'' on page 6)

Classic teddy bear

TWO CLASSIC TOYS dream together in a rocking chair. The doll is from yesterday, but you can make the bear right now.

A child's teddy bear is likely to be a constant companion for years. Soft, brown, warm, and wooly, the bear has been a favorite of children for generations. He picked up his nickname as recently as the Teddy Roosevelt era, but his popularity in folklore goes back for centuries.

Sew our classic bear to last a long time—chances are he'll become a keepsake to hand down from children to grandchildren.

Note: You'll have to fit together a number of curved pieces to make his head and body. For a neat and shapely result, be sure to baste all seams before final stitching.

You'll need: For a 21-inch bear — 1 yard of 45-inch-wide fake fur; 2 contrasting felt squares for paws and soles of feet; scrap of black felt or black embroidery floss for nose; buttons for eyes; thread or dental floss; curved upholstery needle; contrasting embroidery floss for mouth; 2 bags polyester stuffing; ten 2½-inch jar lids; ten ½-inch washers; five ¼-inch by 1½-inch bolts and nuts for swivel joints.

Putting him together

1) Enlarge and transfer patterns (right). Make templates (see page 12). Cut body, head, and limb pieces from fake fur (see page 12 on cutting fake fur). Cut soles and paws from felt.

2) Join 4 head pieces right sides together as shown in sketches 1 and 2, right (all seams are ¼"). Stitch chin gusset to sides between A and B; stitch center gusset to sides between A and C leaving one seam open to neck 5" from C. Clip where indicated.

3) Join 4 body pieces right sides together, leaving 1 seam open between notches. Clip curves.

4) Join leg fronts to backs, right sides together, leaving openings between notches at hips and between D and E at feet. Clip where indicated. Matching D and E, stitch felt soles to open bottoms of feet.

5) Join arm fronts to backs right sides together, leaving openings between notches. Clip where indicated. Join ear fronts to backs, leaving straight edges open.

6) Turn everything right side out. Firmly stuff head, ears, and lower portions of limbs. Tuck in raw edges of ears; stitch to head.

7) With body opening at back, make swivel joints to attach head and limbs (directions on page 8). Blindstitch back head seam closed. Finish stuffing limbs and body; stitch up openings.

8) Appliqué felt paws and nose (or satin stitch nose — see page 10 on embroidery). With curved upholstery needle and dental floss, securely attach button eyes, pushing needle back and forth through head between buttons. Embroider mouth, using chain or outline stitch.

Teddy bear: Enlarge on 1″ grid • ¼″ seam allowance (See "Pattern transfer" on page 6)

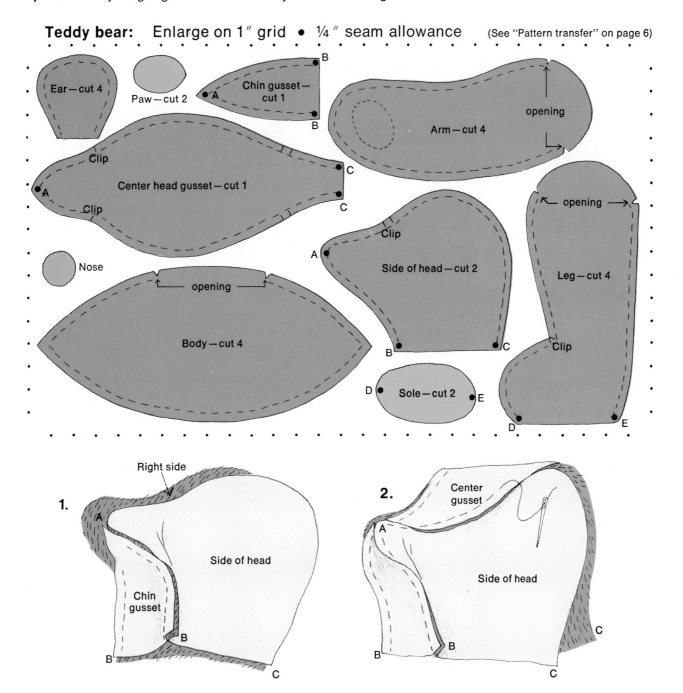

Very scary dragon

Dreadful, dangerous, fire-breathing dragon—you're not really scary. We've transformed your scales into grass-green fur, your flame into an orange felt tongue that licks fingers.

Our famous fairy-tale beast, designed by Francoise Kirkman, is fun for children to team up with a set of toy knights in armor.

You'll need: For 22-inch body — 1 yard 45-inch-wide heavy fabric; 1 felt square for "crest," claws, and pupils of eyes; scraps of yellow and orange felt for flame and nostrils; 2 pompons from curtain fringe for eyes; 1 bag polyester stuffing.

Putting it together

1) Enlarge and transfer pattern (facing page). Cut dragon pieces from fabric, doubled with right sides together. Transfer positions of feet and ears to right side of fabric. Cut "crest" pattern in half and cut from felt square, saving scraps for claws and pupils of eyes. Cut flame from orange and yellow felt. Cut tiny felt circles for eyes and nostrils.

2) As shown in sketch, pin rippled "crest" along right side of 1 side piece (A to D), matching straight edges. Baste close to edge.

3) Baste side pieces, right sides together, along "spine" (A to D), making ¼" seam. Stitch.

4) With right sides facing, pin and baste under-body to sides A and D (it wraps around nose). Stitch, making ¼" seam, leaving 5" opening in 1 side. Turn right side out. Stuff with polyester stuffing. Stitch opening closed.

5) Pair feet pieces. Pin claws around curved edge of right side of each top foot piece, rounded edges of claws facing center of foot. Baste close to edge. With right sides together, sew foot tops to bottoms, leaving straight edges open. Pair and stitch together ears the same way. Turn ears and feet right side out, stuff, and stitch open ends closed. Sew to dragon.

6) Topstitch felt flame pieces together. Stitch securely at mouth. Sew or glue on pompon eyes with felt pupils, and orange felt nostrils.

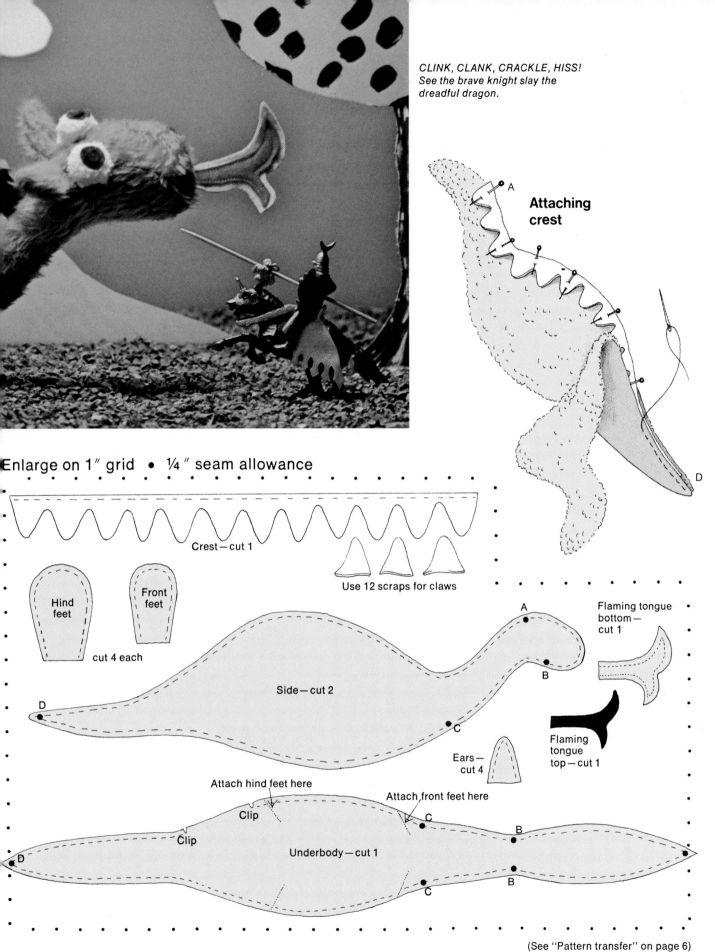

CLINK, CLANK, CRACKLE, HISS!
*See the brave knight slay the
dreadful dragon.*

Attaching crest

A

D

Enlarge on 1″ grid • ¼″ seam allowance

Crest — cut 1

Use 12 scraps for claws

Hind feet

Front feet

cut 4 each

Side — cut 2

A

B

D

C

Flaming tongue bottom — cut 1

Ears — cut 4

Flaming tongue top — cut 1

Attach hind feet here

Attach front feet here

Clip

Clip

C

C

B

B

D

Underbody — cut 1

(See "Pattern transfer" on page 6)

Animals: Very scary dragon   **65**

Soft whimsy

Not everyone is a doll or animal fancier. There are those of us who love the texture of fabric, relish the soft feel of a spongy filling — but would prefer a car or a fried egg to more traditional soft toys. Here we take you further afield than the world of dolls and animals. On the next few pages you'll find a collection of soft toys that range from simple building blocks to a topographical map quilt. We hope they inspire you to have fun creating soft toys of your own.

Village of foam cubes

Here are toys for a junior architect — pretty, squeezable house blocks with removable roofs. An enterprising youngster can stack up an apartment building or arrange a miniature neighborhood, leave rooftops pitched or experiment with new angles.

And Yvonne Emerson's blocks are simple to sew. Use iron-on patches and glued-on floral trimming to make each house go together quickly.

You'll need: Foam cubes, available ready-cut at many outlets (ours are 2 sizes: 4½ inches and 2¼ inches); 9 by 12-inch felt squares (2 for *each* large house, half a square for *each* small house, 2 for *each* large roof, 1 for *each* small roof); electric carving knife, bread knife, or band saw for cutting foam; iron-on patches; floral trimming; white glue or fabric glue; thread to match (or contrast with) felt.

Putting them together

1) Diagonally cut a few small and large cubes to make roofs, using bread knife, band saw, or elec-tric carving knife. Arrange on felt squares, tracing all 5 sides (allow generous overhangs). Cut out, adding wide seam allowance. Trace cube blocks the same way and cut out house sides, floors, and ceilings from felt.

2) Cut up iron-on patches to make appliqué windows, doors, picket fences; bond in place (see package for directions). Cut flowers off floral trimming, and glue in place.

3) Stitch up cube covers, following traced lines — first to join walls, next to attach floor, and finally to attach 1 side of ceiling (see sketches, facing page). Put foam cube inside felt cover; handstitch remaining seam or machine stitch, using zipper foot.

4) Stitch up roof covers, making peak-of-roof seam first, then attaching small triangular pieces to fill in each gable. Put foam block inside roof cover; handstitch bottom piece of felt in place.

Variation: Turn basic cube into alphabet blocks with felt appliqués, or cover foam with crocheted granny squares.

HE RAISES the roof. Maybe it should point the other way? Or come off altogether? Multiple choices are his with a set of house blocks.

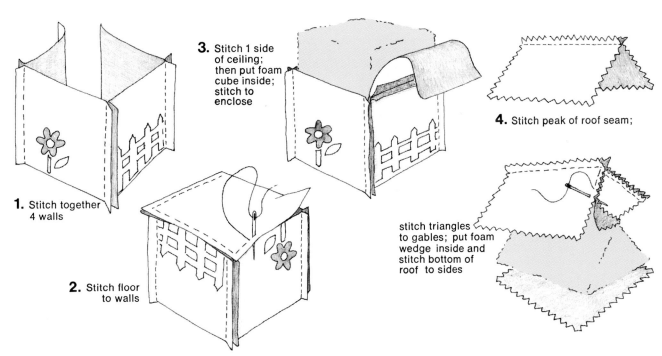

1. Stitch together 4 walls

2. Stitch floor to walls

3. Stitch 1 side of ceiling; then put foam cube inside; stitch to enclose

4. Stitch peak of roof seam;

stitch triangles to gables; put foam wedge inside and stitch bottom of roof to sides

Animal foot cozies

(Photos on page 70)

If you like to kick up your heels occasionally, maybe you need some really chic footwear—like a pair of wild animal slippers. Warm enough for freezing January, soft enough to pamper the tenderest toes, our quilted slippers are also surprisingly simple to make. We offer three creatures (in pairs)—romping rabbits, dashing dachshunds, and beguiling bears—all designed by Francoise Kirkman. To stock your closet or your gift list with further species, just alter ears and tails.

You'll need: For *each* pair — ⅝ yard of 45-inch-wide sturdy cotton or cotton blend fabric (you can substitute wool for luxury, but if you do, have slippers dry-cleaned); ⅝ yard of coordinating lining fabric; eight 6-inch-square cotton scraps for padded legs; solid-color fabric scraps or felt for noses and eyes; thread to match fabrics; 4 buttons for pupils of eyes; 8 white pompons (from curtain fringe) for 2 rabbits' tails; 1 bag polyester quilt batting.

Putting them together

1) Before transferring pattern, measure sole length of a shoe that fits well. Divide this figure by 5 to get size of grid square on which to transfer pattern (if measurement comes out to a fraction, round off to nearest ⅛").

2) Rule correct grid on paper (or use printed graph paper of correct size). Enlarge and transfer pattern (see page 71). Cut 4 body pieces, 4 ear pieces, and 2 sole pieces *each* from body and lining fabrics. For bear, trace body pattern to make nose pattern. Cut 4 nose pieces from lining or other contrasting fabric scraps. Cut dog's nose tip and collar from contrasting scraps.

3) Sketches 1-3 (opposite) show how to make padded legs. Baste 6″ cotton square to wrong side of each body piece, 1 for each leg. On right side, lightly mark outlines of front and back legs, keeping marks at least ⅛″ inside basting. Using contrasting thread, machine stitch over outlines. Turn to wrong side again; remove basting. Using pencil or crochet hook, stuff each leg to make it bulge. Trim away excess cotton scrap close to stitched outline.

4) For each *bear,* press under ¼″ along straight edges of nose pieces. Topstitch close to pressed edge to attach to each body piece where indicated on pattern. Baste along curved edges.

5) To join all slippers, stitch body pieces, right sides together, from A to B (all seams in slipper body are ½″). Repeat for lining pieces. Press seams open. With right sides together, stitch lining to each body around slipper opening (B to C and back to B as in sketch 4 (opposite). Stitch again to reinforce corner at C; clip corner. Turn right side out and press.

6) Topstitch from A to B close to seam of rabbit and bear, close to top of dog's tail (see sketch 5, opposite)—to stabilize heel and hold body and lining together during stuffing.

7) With right sides together, baste and stitch each body around head from C to D, joining all 4 thicknesses. Trim seam; clip curves and corners. Turn to right side; reinforce point C with a few handstitches.

8) To make each sole, place layer of batting between wrong sides of sole and lining pieces. Baste all 3 layers together. With right sides together, matching A and D, stitch sole to body, leaving seam open between notches on *both* sides. Trim seam; turn right side out. Using dowel or crochet hook, stuff each slipper. Blindstitch openings closed.

9) Pair and stitch together ears and bear's tail (we used lining fabric for inside of each ear, body fabric for outside; our bear's tail is entirely body fabric). Turn pieces right side out and stuff. Tuck raw edges to inside; blindstitch openings closed. Securely stitch ears and bear's tail in place.

Appliqué bear's and dog's nose tips and dog's collar. Sew on clusters of 4 pompons for each rabbit's tail. Appliqué felt eyes; sew on button pupils.

(Continued on next page)

Steps in making slippers

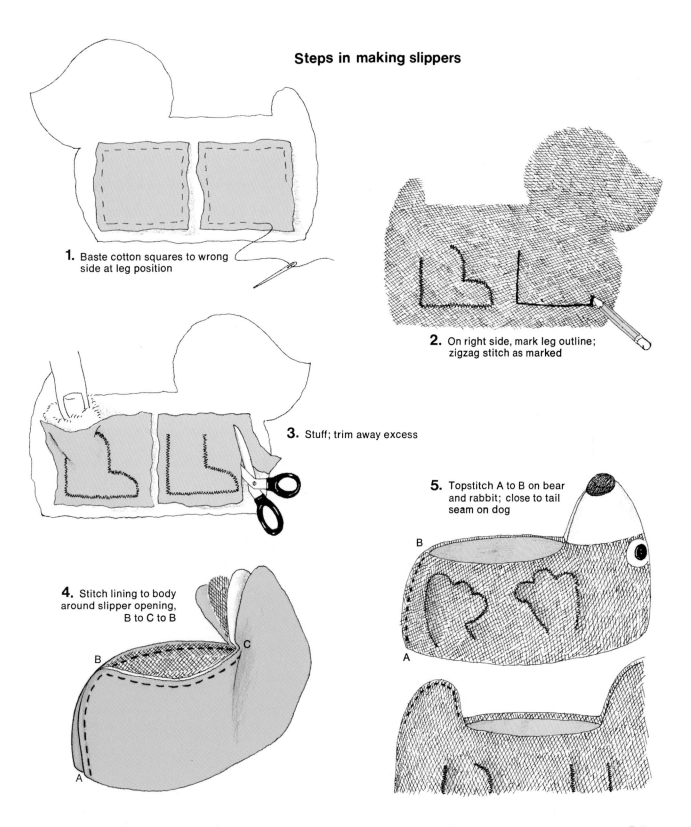

1. Baste cotton squares to wrong side at leg position

2. On right side, mark leg outline; zigzag stitch as marked

3. Stuff; trim away excess

4. Stitch lining to body around slipper opening, B to C to B

5. Topstitch A to B on bear and rabbit; close to tail seam on dog

Whimsy: Foot cozies **69**

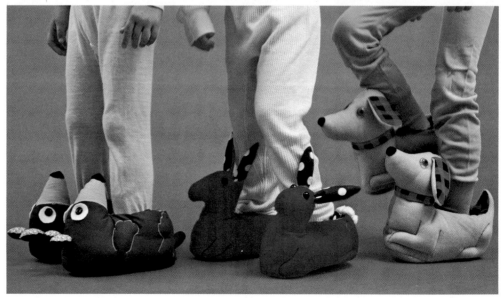

SNUGGLE YOUR TOOTSIES inside a pair of animal slippers. The bears grin up at you (or down, if your feet are in the air). The dachshunds and rabbits watch the road ahead. Directions begin on page 68.

Whimsy: Foot cozies

Animal Foot Cozies: ½ " seam allowance

See step 1 for grid size

(See "Pattern transfer" on page 6)

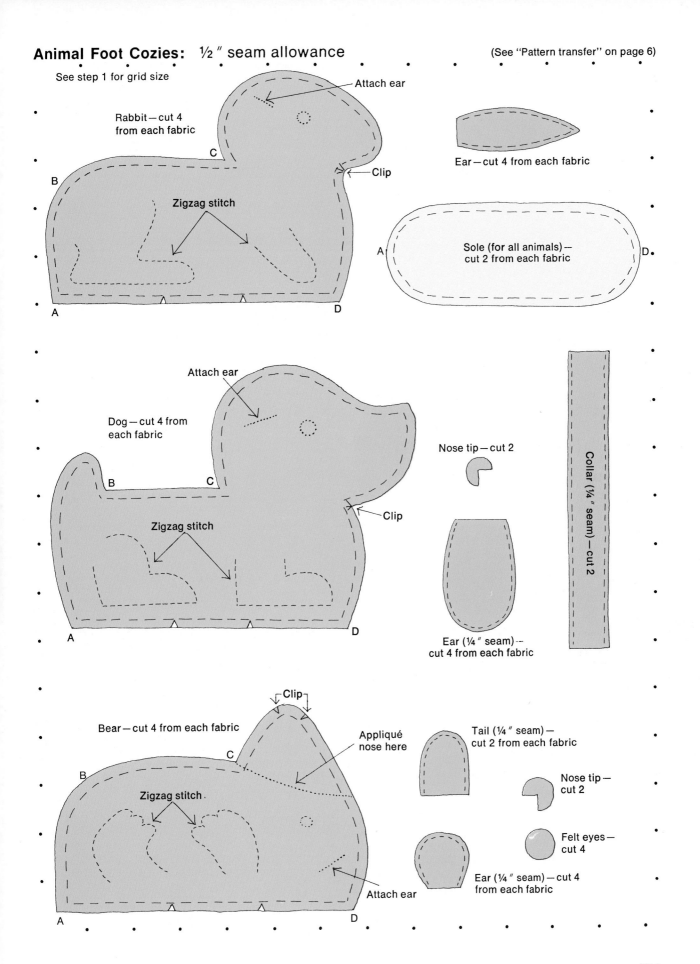

Attach ear

Rabbit — cut 4 from each fabric

C

B

Zigzag stitch

Clip

A

D

Ear — cut 4 from each fabric

Sole (for all animals) — cut 2 from each fabric

A

D

Attach ear

Dog — cut 4 from each fabric

B

C

Zigzag stitch

Clip

A

D

Nose tip — cut 2

Ear (¼ " seam) — cut 4 from each fabric

Collar (¼ " seam) — cut 2

Clip

Bear — cut 4 from each fabric

B

C

Zigzag stitch

Appliqué nose here

A

D

Attach ear

Tail (¼ " seam) — cut 2 from each fabric

Nose tip — cut 2

Felt eyes — cut 4

Ear (¼ " seam) — cut 4 from each fabric

Cuddly cars

BEEP, BEEP! Watch out, orange van. But even if these cars do bump noses, nobody gets hurt —they're made of squishy foam.

Most cars, even toy ones, eventually break down. These don't. You can't even mar their pretty paint — if you poke them, they just squish. In a collision, these classy concoctions of foam and felt are as safe as bumper cars.

And they're styled to suit various breeds of car buff: one satisfied owner cushions her back against a soft sedan while driving a real car; another owner, age 4, takes his cuddly coupe to bed. Our three colorful cars are the work of Ruth Law.

You'll need: Wide wrapping paper for pattern; 1 yard felt for *each* car plus 4 black felt squares for wheels; oblong pieces of foam (we used blocks 2 feet by 1 foot by 4 inches); electric knife, bread knife, or band saw for cutting foam; white

felt squares or iron-on patches for contrasting windows, white walls, license plates; thread to match felt as well as to contrast for zigzag stitched trim; narrow, shiny white cord for extra trim; scraps of hardboard for wheels.

Putting them together

1) Working on large sheet of paper, custom-design a car, bus, or truck. Draw side view only, keeping lines simple (vehicle will be carved out of foam — a wobbly job). Cut out your drawing.

2) Lay drawing on flat side of foam block; trace with black felt-tip pen. Draw lines across block at points where angles will be carved. Turn block

over; place drawing on reverse side, aligning it with lines drawn across block. Carve, following tracing, using bread knife, band saw, or electric carving knife.

3) With knife or saw, cut out 4 circles of hardboard for wheels. Trace wheels on felt squares, folded in half. Cut out, adding ample seam allowance. Trace and cut out felt body the same way. Using tape measure, find out distance around outside edge of car body. Cut strip or strips of felt as long as this measurement and 5″ wide.

4) Decorate sides of vehicle with fine cord. Cut out iron-on patch windows and bond to felt (see package for directions). With felt pen, draw people in windows, if desired.

5) Piece together sections of felt center strip, if necessary. Topstitch all seams, trimming away seam allowance afterwards. Pin strip to 1 side piece, following traced line, leaving underbody loose. Stitch as pinned.

6) With foam shape inside, pin 2nd side to center strip, adjusting seam allowance of strip to fit snugly and pinning over traced line on side piece. Leave underbody loose and remove foam shape. Stitch as pinned. Put foam shape back inside; lay underbody strip in place (trimming away excess); handstitch to close.

7) Sandwich hardboard wheels between 2 felt circles. Using zipper foot, stitch around perimeter. Handstitch wheels to car.

Balanced diet mobile

Suspend a flutter of color in the kitchen—make a favorite foods mobile to cheer up the cook, to whet the family's appetite, to amuse the baby, or just to celebrate good food.

We stitched each food from felt squares, available in an appetizing array of colors from salmon pink to rich spinach green. We chose our favorite foods, trying to keep the diet balanced—and colorful.

You'll need: One 8½ by 11-inch felt square for *every* 1 or 2 foods (we used 2 bright green squares and 1 *each* of bright yellow, pale yellow, yellow orange, bright orange, salmon pink, shocking pink, purple pink, bright red, white, chartreuse, beige, and medium brown, plus tiny scraps of black for watermelon seeds); spools of thread both to match and to contrast with felt; 3½ yards of ½-inch-wide grosgrain ribbon (measured to hang mobile from 8-foot ceiling); 10-inch wooden embroidery hoop; 3-inch wooden ring (curtain ring or purse handle sold at fabric shops); dental floss; white, red, and brown embroidery floss.

Putting it together

1) Enlarge and transfer patterns (facing page), or substitute your own favorite food. Trace patterns for egg, cheese, bread loaf, pea pod, and watermelon to make patterns of their appliquéd felt details.

2) After folding each felt square in half widthwise, arrange and pin patterns and tracing of appliqués on felt of appropriate color. Cut through both thicknesses of felt so you have a front and a back for each food and 2 of each appliqué. Lightly transfer guidelines for machine embroidery to front and back of salmon, bread loaf, tomato, corn, lettuce, and artichoke—unless you prefer freehand embroidery (transfer techniques are described on page 12).

3) After pinning fronts to backs, stitch close to edge of orange, milk bottle, potato, and apple (insert apple's leaf before finishing seam). Take a few stitches with white embroidery floss to indicate potato eyes.

4) Pin fronts to backs of artichoke, lettuce, corn, fish, banana, carrot, tomato, and beet. Stitch close to edge of each, inserting tops of carrot and beet before finishing seams. Using contrasting thread and zigzag stitching, machine embroider details on corn kernels, artichokes and lettuce leaves, fish fins and scales, and carrot, beet, and tomato "ribs." (Machine embroidery is explained on page 9. Practice on scraps first to find stitch width you like.)

5) Arrange appliqués on both fronts and backs of cheese, bread, egg, pea pod, and watermelon. Stitch in place. Match fronts to backs and stitch together as you stitched foods mentioned previously. With contrasting thread, zigzag stitch bread loaf to indicate slash lines in top. Take stitches with brown embroidery floss to make grains in sliced end. Glue on black watermelon seeds (or embroider, or mark with black felt-tip pen).

6) Cut 1½ yards of ribbon. Loop through small wood ring and attach ends to ceiling so that ring hangs comfortably within reach. Cut remaining ribbon in half. Using macramé mounting knot (shown in sketches 1-4, opposite page), link each remaining ribbon at its center to hanging ring (4 equal lengths should hang down).

7) Take apart embroidery hoop (set aside outer hoop with screw attachment). Pass end of each ribbon under inner hoop, from outside to inside; pin ribbon to itself to make short loop around hoop. Adjust pins until all 4 ribbons are taut and evenly spaced and hoop is horizontal.

8) Thread each felt food on length of dental floss and tie securely to hoop, balancing weights, colors, and shapes. After making last adjustments, handstitch ribbons securely where pinned.

Variation: Suspend felt animals from ribbons as in a carousel.

ANYBODY HUNGRY? Sunny-side-up egg and other delicacies float in a kitchen mobile.

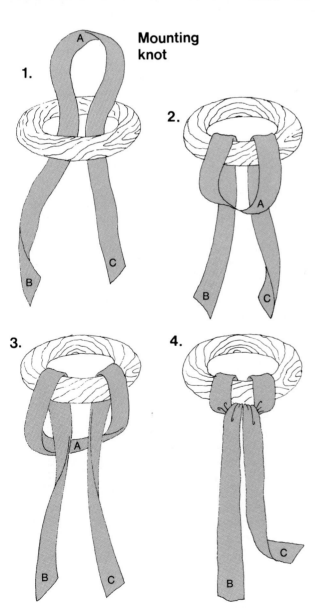

Mounting knot

1.

2.

3.

4.

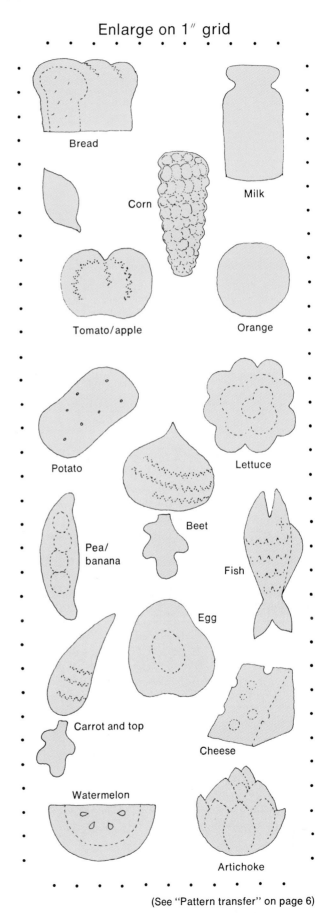

Enlarge on 1″ grid

Bread

Milk

Corn

Tomato/apple

Orange

Potato

Lettuce

Beet

Pea/banana

Fish

Egg

Carrot and top

Cheese

Watermelon

Artichoke

(See "Pattern transfer" on page 6)

Nap map

(Photo on page 78)

I was the giant great and still
That sits upon the pillow-hill
And sees before him, dale and plain,
The pleasant land of counterpane.
　　　　　　　—Robert Louis Stevenson

Like Stevenson's counterpane, our topographical quilt invites hours of fantasy in a miniature world. When the "giant" feels sleepy, he can rest his head on one of the hill pillows and curl up on soft velour meadows, lake, and roadway.

Our map, designed by Barbara Benson, roughly resembles the landscape just north of San Francisco (see page 78). But if you prefer some other region—real or imaginary—just alter the appliqués.

You'll need: For a 50-inch square quilt with 2 hill pillows—2½ yards of 54 to 60-inch-wide beige cotton velour (or similar fabric) for background; ¾ yard blue velour for sea; ¾ yard green velour for meadows; ¾ yard orange felt for road (we chose orange for brightness, but you could substitute black felt or wet-look vinyl); 2¼ yards of 70-inch-wide preshrunk muslin for lining; 1 square *each* brown and black felt for trees and road divider strip (substitute white if road is black); ¼ yard *each* of 5 rainbow colors of velveteen tubing to outline tunnel; scraps of green cotton prints and solids for trees; thread to match fabrics; button thread or crochet twine; 1 curtain weight for *each* tree; two 12-ounce juice cans or 10-inch mailing tube for tunnel; 10-inch and 8½-inch mixing bowls; 4 yards polyester quilt batting (or 1 package); 1 bag shredded foam.

Putting it together

1) Enlarge map design (opposite page) and transfer to 50″ paper square. Go over outlines with black felt-tip pen. To make patterns for sea and meadow appliqués, trace labeled areas, adding ½″ all around for seam allowance. Enlarge and transfer roadway pattern (beneath map).

2) Cut one 52″ square *each* from muslin and beige velour. Cut meadow appliqués from green velour, sea from blue. Tucking under ½″ all around, pin and appliqué meadows and sea to beige background where indicated on pattern. Cut road segments (A through H) from orange felt. Arrange to cover stitching of sea and meadow; pin and appliqué.

3) Cut 2 layers of quilt batting (52″ square) to cover muslin square (for optional sculptured hills, add extra pieces of batting over base layers). Smooth beige quilt top over muslin lining and batting. Pin layers together 2″ from edges all around. Take several long basting stitches across quilt to prevent layers from slipping when you machine stitch. Turn raw edges to inside, making 1″ hem with mitered corners. Quilt with wide zigzag stitch, following edges of appliqués.

4) From muslin, construct each hill pillow of 2 circles — a top and a base. Base circles are 8½″ and 10″ in diameter (trace the mixing bowls). Tops are 14″ and 17″. Drape 14″ circle over smaller bowl and 17″ circle over larger bowl. As shown in sketch 1 on page 79, pin darts to fit evenly around bowl rims; stitch darts in place. Drape layer of quilt batting over each; stitch in place, easing in fullness at base. (When pillow is finished, batting will be inside.) Remove bowls. Turn domes right side out.

5) To make tunnel, remove ends of juice cans and tape and glue securely end-to-end (or substitute mailing tube cut to 9½″). Slice off 2½″ along 1 side of tube. Glue and tape cardboard strip 2½ by 10″ into sliced opening (see sketch 2 on page 79). Line curve of tunnel (not roadway) with glued black felt or vinyl, allowing ½″ extra at each end. After glue is dry, trace tunnel entrances with pencil at opposite sides of larger muslin hill 1″ from base edge. Staystitch over tracings. Cut out holes ¼″ inside stitching. Clip around curve and tuck raw edge inside (see sketch 3 on page 79).

(Continued on page 78)

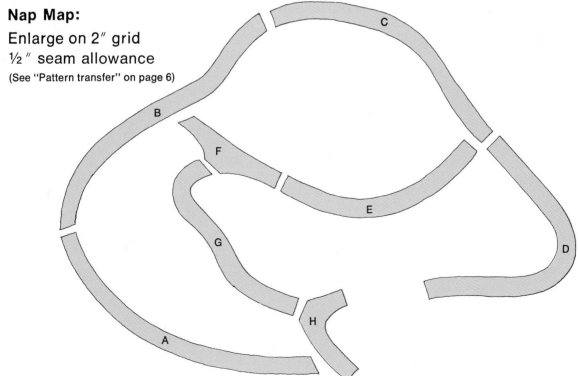

Nap Map:

Enlarge on 2″ grid
½ ″ seam allowance

(See "Pattern transfer" on page 6)

. . . Nap map (cont'd.)

6) Pin hill domes to corresponding bases, right sides together; stitch, leaving 6″ open. Turn right side out. Fit tunnel into larger pillow. Whipstitch around entrances, joining muslin to tunnel lin-ing. Fill both pillows with shredded foam (use large funnel or paper cone to reduce mess; see page 6 for other suggestions). Stitch openings closed.

BOATS in the bay, cars on the road. Our landscape quilt with hill pillows provides a soft backdrop for hours of fantasy. Directions start on page 76.

7) To slipcover both pillows, cut out 4 circles of beige velour, each 2″ larger in diameter than the 4 muslin circles cut out in step 4. Hem the 2 largest circles ½″. Make drawstrings on right side of each by catching 60″ lengths of button thread or crochet twine under wide zigzag stitches close to edge (see sketch 4). Pull drawstring of larger pillow to fit over top and sides of tunnel pillow, leaving base uncovered (it should look baggy). Mark tunnel entrances ½″ above drawstring. Remove slipcover; cut out and finish as you did entrances in muslin pillow (see step 5). Slipstitch rainbow stripes of velveteen tubing to arc over entrance (see sketch 5).

Put slipcover back on tunnel pillow, lining up entrances. Pull drawstring, tie, and tuck inside. Tuck raw edge of velour base inside; slipstitch to velour dome. Join smaller slipcovered pillow to its base the same way.

8) To make tree trunks, cut out 4″ square of brown felt for *each*. Fold in half; seam 4″ edges, forming tube. Cut out small circle to fit 1 opening of tube; handstitch in place. Fill with sand or place curtain weight in base; stuff. To make treetops and bushes, cut out 6″-diameter circles of print fabric. Gather edges and fill with stuffing. Pull gathers tight and knot thread to enclose. Sew treetops to trunks as shown in sketch 6.

Variation: Design quilt using bird's-eye view of city or neighborhood. Use foam houses, page 66, to finish urban landscape.

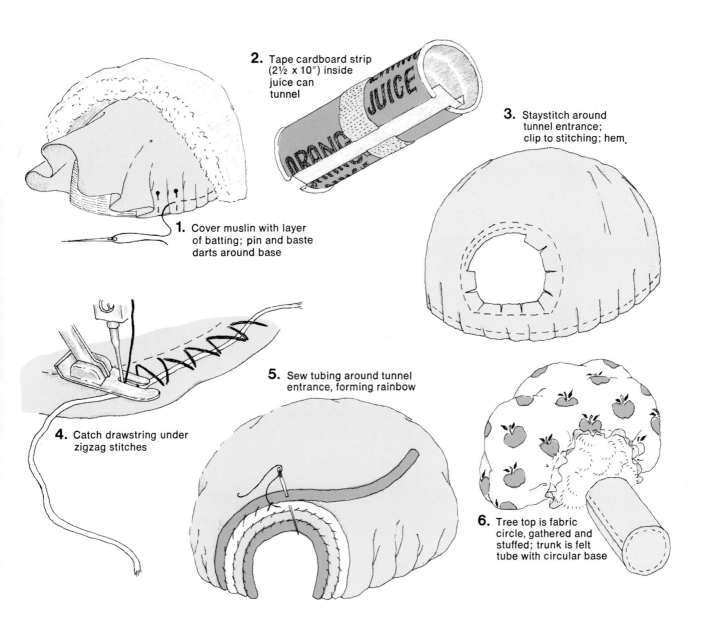

1. Cover muslin with layer of batting; pin and baste darts around base

2. Tape cardboard strip (2½ x 10″) inside juice can tunnel

3. Staystitch around tunnel entrance; clip to stitching; hem.

4. Catch drawstring under zigzag stitches

5. Sew tubing around tunnel entrance, forming rainbow

6. Tree top is fabric circle, gathered and stuffed; trunk is felt tube with circular base

Index

Waking/sleeping dolls, page 21.